THE GOLDEN FIVE
FRAMEWORK

Harnessing Five Essential
Types of Marketing for Success
in the 21st Century

JACQUELINE S. RUIZ

CEO, JJR Marketing / Fig Factor Media

THE GOLDEN FIVE
FRAMEWORK

For more information, contact:

Fig Factor Media, LLC | www.figfactormedia.com

Cover Design & Layout by Juan Pablo Ruiz
Printed in the United States of America

ISBN: 978-1-957058-71-9
Library of Congress Control Number: 2022914720

FIG
FACTOR
MEDIA

DEDICATION

This book is dedicated to every business seeking results from their marketing efforts

When I hear the word "marketing," I find it synonymous with the word "magic."

CONTENTS

INTRO

JACQUELINE S. RUIZ
ENTREPRENEUR, AUTHOR,
SPEAKER, PHILANTHROPIST,
PILOT.

When I hear the word "marketing," I find it synonymous with the word "magic." That's because I am eternally impressed by how the right campaign, content, and/or idea can profoundly affect our businesses, communities, and individuals.

Why is this? Because in my opinion, marketing creates an incredibly visceral experience that is shared across every industry and nonprofit. Every organization needs marketing. So, if you can connect your marketing with organizations on a deeper level, the result will be amazing.

I've spent half of my life as a marketing consultant and chief executive officer (CEO), making sure that my client's products and services were no well-kept secret. What started as a career in marketing for a hospitality chain (and then a chain of Brazilian restaurants) grew into the launch of an award-winning marketing agency, JJR Marketing, in 2006. We've become a conduit for creating brands and campaigns that are innovative and measurably effective for clients.

Since then, I've launched scores of brands, advised thousands of clients on their marketing goals, reaped numerous awards, launched several nonprofits, and founded a publishing company where I have authored twenty-six books in addition to this one. Yet I would never call marketing, in any sense of the word, an "easy" venture.

I see marketing as an incredible combination of science, strategy, and art, taking many forms to create the best possible outcome for our clients. **There's no magic pill, but the closest thing I've found is the Golden Five Framework**—the five types of marketing that can reach within the overcrowded headspace of those in our target market and touch their souls. I share a long history of success with these five, never-fail types of marketing. It's time to unleash this paradigm to the world, and I'm confident that if we all use them correctly, we can connect to people's hearts and awaken people's minds to take action, even in the somewhat cynical, challenging landscape of the 21st century. Along the way we'll also inspire and impact others to bring the magic forward, connect with others, and help them as well. I believe marketing is more than a class in college or a sign in a store. It's a living, breathing way to impact the world by helping people make the right decisions.

May the Golden Five Framework positively impact those most important to you.

—Jacqueline S. Ruiz

PART ONE

MARKETING IN THE 21ST CENTURY

CHAPTER 1

THE CHALLENGE OF THE 21ST CENTURY MARKETER

If you work in marketing, you know that you work in a constantly changing industry. In fact, it may be part of the appeal for you. I know it is for me.

Marketing is dynamic, and typically, no two days are the same. Marketers love to affect change. And while the need for companies to get their message across to their audiences will always be with us, the ways in which we can do it is always in flux and heavily influenced by many factors, especially technology, resources, and even world events!

Perhaps you've been working in the industry long enough to remember the days before social media, or even the dawning of Google. If not, here's a brief history lesson on the evolution of marketing.

Before the majority of our marketing was done digitally, there were fewer choices available to marketers who needed to communicate with their audiences. In fact, there was a very short list of marketing vehicles to use, and they all involved a marketer reaching out to their target audience in broadcast or print media, on billboards, or with direct mail. Marketing methods of the past included such methods as:

- Newspaper and magazine advertising
- Direct mail
- Flyers and handbills
- Billboards
- Radio and TV advertising
- Trade shows
- Public and private special events

Yes, we realize that many of these traditional methods still have value to businesses today. However, for the majority of businesses, the list is far too limited and somewhat ineffective for their needs. When computers began to show up in consumer homes, soon followed by ubiquitous internet access, the world opened up for marketers everywhere. In 1991, researchers broadcast a pot of coffee filling up so they could tell when a fresh pot was made without having to leave their desks. The broadcast ended up being the first webcam (Pew Research 2014) and spoke to how the internet could serve our everyday needs. In 1994, the term "surfing the net" was coined and 11 million households had internet access. Soon, the White House joined them, and the first known web purchase—a pepperoni pizza—was ordered from Pizza Hut. (Pew Research 2014). In what is now a historic event, Google.com registered as a domain on September 15, 1997. (Leswing 2017) By the year 2000, 48 percent of internet users had purchased a product online. (Pew Research 2014)

Then in 2004, Mark Zuckerberg launched Facebook and signed up 1,200 Harvard students in the first twenty-four hours, eventually giving rise to an innovative way to market to people. Social media gave marketers everywhere a truly personal and targeted way to reach their markets. Facebook led to many more social media platforms that began to compete for our advertising dollars.

As the internet added a whole new list of opportunities for marketers, the traditional ways remained, but began to wane in popularity. Ways of reaching consumers via the internet are expanding every day and include:

Marketers love to affect change.

- Social media
- E-commerce
- Company websites
- Content marketing (blogs and articles)
- Online and in-app sites
- Google Ads
- Pay-per-click advertising
- Search engine optimization
- Search engine marketing
- Online media sites
- Email marketing
- Podcasts and streamed content

The internet opened up a special channel of communication between the consumer and the marketer. Now, consumers search for very specific, targeted information about the products and services they want. On the marketer's side, the internet offers options to post content and other data that can be searched by the consumer. **Instead of the marketer always having to "reach out" to the consumer, the consumer could now welcome "in" content from the marketer on their computer screen, thanks to the internet.**

INBOUND VERSUS OUTBOUND MARKETING

The rise of websites and social media shifted marketing gradually from a traditional outbound (or "push") model to an inbound or "pull" one. As their names imply, "inbound" and "outbound" marketing are two different marketing methods. In outbound marketing, companies push their ads out to the consumer without their active consent or solicitation. For example, we do not request those printed ads that fill our mailboxes, nor the billboard that looms over us during our morning commute, the ad that interrupts our magazine story, or the commercial we must sit through before our free video streams. These push tactics are unsolicited attempts to reach out to us. Many of the marketing vehicles in the "traditional list" fit this model. This type of outbound marketing is a one-way street since only one of the parties involved is truly invested in the message being received—and that's the sender!

Inbound, or pull marketing, is exactly the opposite. The term was coined by Brian Halligan, HubSpot co-founder and CEO, in 2005 to describe the marketing that the consumer invites into their world, through opt-in or internet search. (Jacobson 2019) It's a marketing strategy that aligns with your audience, by creating and distributing valuable content that they need and want, when they request it or search for it. For example, instead of placing an ad for a new lawn mower, the manufacturer may publish an article or guide about how to pick the best lawnmower for their needs. **This kind of valuable content is wanted and searched for by consumers, and welcomed "in" to their Google searches; hence the term, "inbound marketing."** Many times, consumers even "opt in" to receive inbound marketing material, like a subscription to an e-newsletter or access to a special guide or list. It's another form of inbound marketing.

After the internet sparked this marketing milieu, consumers took control of how they were going to find information on the products and services they needed. Companies sat up, paid attention and turned their focus from producing ads (an outbound technique) to producing and publishing valuable content that a consumer could search for on the internet, like blogs and articles about products and services (the pull technique).

Inbound marketing is effective because the communication is wanted; both the sender and the recipient have an interest. It's a symbiotic relationship, a two-way street where the sender provides the communication that the recipient seeks and finds. Once they do, the grateful consumer may learn enough to buy into an offer or make a purchase. In other words, the enlightened consumer of today demands more than just advertisements. They want education. Pull marketing works because it provides what they need, and will continue to need in the ever-changing and growing marketplace.

It's interesting to note that as the distribution

of printed, written content has embraced the inbound marketing model, so has the entertainment industry. When television and radio first began, you would turn on the station and hear something being broadcast, whether it be a talk show or an advertisement, whether you wanted to hear it or not. Now we control the entertainment that comes into our house. We pay for subscription streaming services to choose what we want. We hear our favorite song or playlist any time we want, if not from the downloaded music on our phone, then through Spotify or a different streaming service. Today, podcasts have replaced talk radio because we can choose the shows we want, add them to our playlist, and get information on the hyper-specific topics we're interested in, from last night's episode of our favorite Netflix series to the latest trends in our professional industry.

Yet, as in most things within the marketing, there is no one-size-fits-all approach in the 21st century. For example, you would think that every small business has a website but that's not true. Forty-six percent of small businesses do not have

a website. An article from PC Magazine from 2021 reported that more than 29 percent of small businesses do not have a website. Why? The top reason was that social media generated enough business to satisfy their needs, while others just said they've never needed one, are focused on a niche, or have customers that don't go online to find them. (Rist 2021) In other words, some marketers buck the rules and succeed, even though studies support the overwhelming evidence that consumers begin their buying journey at the computer with a Google search. In fact, one study showed that 70-80 percent of consumers research a small business before making a purchase, and of those businesses who employ websites, 92 percent of them believe having a website contributes effectively to their digital marketing strategy. (A. 2022)

Then there are digital ads that reach us as we are searching the net. I consider these hybrids between the push and pull marketing efforts. For example, have you ever looked at an item online and then had ads about it "follow you around" whenever you are searching for competing products? With the insertion of a simple tracking code on their website, a company that we visit online can track our website behavior and "retarget" their advertising to us. Their ads can "follow us" on the internet and remind us of an item's special benefit, or inform us of a sale price to give us one more chance to buy, even when we are perusing the website of a competing store. Although we may not appreciate every digital ad we see, they are almost always generated only after we've gone to a site and researched a specific item on our own. In other words, we indirectly "requested" the ad (a pull technique) by showing interest in the product. **The number of times we continue to see it before we actually buy the product is a push effort on the part of the company to get us back onto their site and into the shopping cart!**

THE BIGGEST CHALLENGES

The rise of technology in the marketing industry has brought wonderful developments but also has brought along with it a new, menacing hurdle—the cacophony of communication in the marketplace. **Today, it's becoming increasingly difficult to stand out among the many other messages bombarding consumers every day.** In 2021, that number has been reported as 10,000 messages daily—a 50 percent increase from 2007, according to some studies. (whoofey.com n.d.) In addition to this daily overdose of information, today's consumer is a tougher customer. Armed with the internet and more information than ever before, consumers can't be fooled. With ever-evolving technology and changing societal factors, today's marketers must cater to the savvy consumers of today. The obstacles to winning them over are many, varied, and unique to the human race in the 21st century. Here are the main ones.

Today's marketers have to do in seconds what they could do in minutes years ago.

OVERCOMING THE CONSUMER'S DWINDLING ATTENTION SPAN

I personally believe that today's marketers have to do in seconds what they could do in minutes years ago. It's no secret that as a society, we have incredibly short attention spans. As social media platforms developed, restrictions on message length did too because social media marketers understood this. That's the reason for Twitter's 280-character count and TikTok's original ten-second time length. It's enough communication to sufficiently get a point across to our impatient brains. And judging by the popularity of those platforms, nobody is arguing. It all makes sense. If we are going to process even part of the 10,000 marketing messages we see daily, we can't spend too much time on each one, can we?

A mentor once told me that one of the biggest gifts marketers have is the ability to synthesize information into the bite-sized pieces that resonate with people. With everything we are exposed to—from the time we wake up until the time our heads hit the pillow—people don't have the time and attention span to absorb everything most companies want to say. If the "headline" or "main message" appeals, they will scroll down, read the ad, listen to the podcast, or turn their attention to the paragraphs of content set before them. But it has to resonate. The lesson here? As marketers, we have to get to the point—and quickly!

COMPANIES MUST EARN CUSTOMER LOYALTY

Customer loyalty is a rare thing these days.

The customer of the 21st century is discriminating and demanding. They research, read online reviews, check out return policies, and expect delivery as promised. They research price differences on products and services with the click of a button. If you want to beat the low-price leader, you'll have to offer something better, and of value, like customer service, an advantageous return policy or a customer loyalty special. You also must perform with integrity. **If your company doesn't keep its promises, the consumer will move on to the next service provider that offers a better price, has better reviews, or promises better service.** If you are in the unfortunate position of disappointing a customer, you could easily drive them to leave a negative review. This can have untold, snowballing consequences without you ever knowing it.

Another reason customer loyalty is at a premium is the rise in customer skepticism. Some people won't believe your reviews or even what you say. They demand to do their own research. In 2022, this was echoed in the political sphere and the cries of "fake news!" The internet has provided opportunity for plenty of scams and nobody wants to be burned twice. Although studies show that a high percentage (about 80 percent) of consumers believe online reviews, an even higher percentage (97 percent) is watching to make sure the company responds to any negative review. (Lin 2021) Customers don't give their loyalty; they expect companies to earn it.

COMPANIES MUST DIFFERENTIATE THEMSELVES

As consumers learned to use the internet, a funny thing happened to the businesses trying to sell to them. It became increasingly difficult for businesses to differentiate themselves from the competition. I believe the challenge for today's marketer is a creative one to reach out in a more disruptive, unforgettable way. Using technology is part of this.

For example, ALS will forever be associated with the 2014 Ice Bucket Challenge. The organization challenged people to post a video dumping a bucketful of ice water over their heads to earn donations for ALS. The stunt increased the annual funding for ALS by 187 percent. (ALS Association 2019) On social media, celebrities like Kim Kardashian, Lady GaGa, Leo DeCaprio, Britney Spears and many others posted videos of themselves getting soaked for ALS. (Alexander 2016) They have forever differentiated themselves from other nonprofits—and all it took was a little creativity!

These are all very valid and important obstacles that challenge the 21st marketer today. But there is one other element that is perhaps the most important in helping the small business owner reach their marketing objectives in the 21st century. It can be summarized in one word.

Strategy.

THE FOLLY OF FRAGMENTATION

With all of the ways we can reach out to our audiences these days, from the outbound "oldies but goodies" to the "latest and greatest" inbound techniques, it is easier than ever to fragment our efforts as a business. I've seen small businesses whose social media accounts look nothing like their website, down to a different version of the logo or a dramatically different tone in how they address the reader. I've seen companies send out monthly eblasts to their customers without thinking to share the latest blog or new product announcement.

Fragmentation of marketing efforts is the enemy of your return on investment (ROI). I've learned from experience and from working with clients who come to me with fragmented efforts that the best results come from a cohesive, integrated approach to marketing. If you are whiteboarding the ways you are communicating to your customers, and some of the marketing channels are not "talking" to the others, your efforts are fragmented and you are missing opportunities.

At JJR Marketing, I find that people either call me for strategy because they know they need one, or they come in confused, not understanding why their efforts are not working. In both cases, I provide them what they need, which is a sound marketing strategy. Sometimes for the strategy to work in their environment, we have some obstacles to overcome. These are important to identify at the outset of our engagement. **Sometimes, the remedies are not straightforward, or even available.** However, it's important for everyone to agree on the restrictions going in. That way

everyone agrees on the obstacles they need to overcome, and the best possible strategy can be developed. What are these obstacles in our businesses that keep our marketing fragmented and ineffective? While every company is different, I repeatedly see some of the same roadblocks.

LACK OF TALENT

Too often, marketing efforts fall to the owner of the company or his/her assistant. It soon becomes a secondary responsibility that often gets bumped when things get busy. For a true marketing strategy to take wings, someone must be dedicated to its implementation. They can be an employee at the firm, or an outsourced professional. **For many companies, this is where a marketing agency can really make a difference and alleviate the burden of managing some or all of their marketing efforts.**

LACK OF DATA

Many companies come to me with a website, but they have never looked at their analytics. They have never taken time to understand how their audience uses their website, what pages appeal to them, and when they click away. One of the greatest advantages of digital marketing is that it is so measurable. Most every marketing platform, from Google Analytics for websites or MailChimp for email marketing, has robust reporting that tells a business what kind of response they are getting. For emails they report the number of opens and views, as well as clickthroughs and shares.

Even if your company is using push marketing efforts, like postcards and ads, you still can monitor whether you are getting leads. Some direct mail programs allow you to replace your real phone number on the ad with a tracking phone number so you can count the calls placed from that dedicated line. QR codes, too, can generate website traffic when it's included on a printed piece and easily monitored if the QR code goes to a specific landing page.

Regardless of how a company is carrying out its marketing strategy, **the more knowledge and data we have about how people respond to marketing efforts, the easier it is to create and implement a marketing strategy.** I often find myself encouraging and educating clients on how best to do this.

LACK OF BUDGET

Every company needs a marketing budget, and the amount of that budget should depend upon the industry and the revenue of the company. A rule of thumb is that the average business spends anywhere from 1-11 percent of their revenue on advertising and marketing, depending on whether the business is a business-to-business (B2B) or business-to-consumer (B2C) business. B2Cs typically have higher budgets, as their audience is typically more widespread. (Lesonsky 2019)

As an agency, I run up against the budget

issue with clients all the time. Marketing is an investment, but one that must be made if goals are to be met. And depending on a variety of factors, it can pay off in leads and conversions many times over the actual investment. With the right talent and data, you can typically monitor the ROI of a marketing program.

LACK OF IMAGINATION

A good marketing strategy encompasses the hopes and dreams of the entrepreneur or the CEO. The dream is typically not in reach, but with the ultimate goal in place, you can take steps in the right direction. In other words, you can't go to the moon if the rocket isn't built, but you can certainly begin work on the engine. By beginning with the big picture, you can break your marketing challenges down into smaller pieces and tackle them one by one. That's what a marketing strategy is all about.

When I begin work on a marketing strategy with a client, I try to get them to **use their**

imagination and really envision something greater than the status quo and what they are doing at the present time. We may or may not be able to reach their goal in the near future, but it gives me direction as I shape their marketing strategy. Then, I just need to develop the steps to get them there.

The Golden Five Framework—Based on the Challenges

My belief in strategy and its importance for the 21st century marketer extends to the Golden Five types of marketing that I discuss in the second half of this book. With an understanding of the consumer mindset of today, I sit down with clients and evaluate the marketing they have in place. Almost always, they are missing one of the five types. And then I know that part of the strategy will be the one that needs the most work. And away we'll go!

However, there's another valuable, yet often missed part of the strategy that's very important to every marketing initiative. **It's called intention.**

CHAPTER 2

MARKETING WITH INTENTION

Business has changed a lot over the years. There was once a time when everyone had an office on Main Street. It was the only way to be taken seriously in the business world. We had business cards and sent out letters on company letterhead. Companies sought high-profile office space addresses and actually *occupied* them instead of just leasing a mailbox there. We dressed up for work and remained there for eight hours, plus a lunch break, before heading home. In those days, when it came to choosing a company to work with, things were WYSIWYG— what you see is what you get.

Then came the internet, and with it, talented web developers and creative people. Now, solopreneurs can look as professional and flashy online as the larger, well-known companies. We check our morning email in our pajamas, take time during the day to drop our children off or go exercise, then work late into the night to get our work done for the next day, and nobody knows the difference. Besides that, (unless we Google it) there is virtually no sure way of knowing from a website how many people are involved with the company, or if it is run from an office space or someone's basement.

Thanks to the internet, many business owners also are no longer limited by their geography, even if their business is based on relationship-building and in-person meetings. They now can pick their favorite online meeting platform and meet virtually. Digital service providers and consultants on the East Coast easily meet weekly to serve their clients on the West Coast. In short, the internet made it easier for us to meet, to sell, and to consult from anywhere in the world to anyone in the world.

WHO IS YOUR CUSTOMER?

This used to be an easier question to answer than it is today. The internet has made our world smaller. We can more effortlessly reach a larger audience. And just as your market has evolved, you can be sure that your target customer's attitude towards your brand has evolved, too.

One reason for this is the changing demographics in the marketplace. Every business has a different audience, but the overall makeup of consumers is changing in the country. Today's consumers are more sophisticated. They also are more demanding of the companies they patronize. Most strikingly, the marketplace has seen a rise in millennials and Generation Z consumers. These two demographic groups (born after 1981) are vastly different from the generations before them because of their digital intelligence and expectations. In 2019, millennials surpassed the baby boomers as the nation's largest living adult generation (Fry 2020) at 72.1 million. So, for marketers in the 21st century, it's smart to know a little bit about them.

Millennials are a new breed of consumer. As they came of age, America experienced 9/11 and an economic recession. As a result, they worry about their day-to-day future, as well as the future of generations and the planet. They are diverse, and open-minded and accepting of other races, gender, sexual orientation, etc. (Comperatore and Nerone 2008)

Millennials are a new breed of consumer.

In terms of their consumer behavior, millennials are friendly to online purchases, but regularly worry about data hacks and internet frauds. Almost half of them (47 percent) live paycheck to paycheck and worry they won't be able to cover their expenses. (The Deloitte Global 2022 GenZ & Millennial Survey 2022) Another distinguishing trait is their social consciousness and commitment to the causes that they value. They are concerned with climate change, renewable energy, and recycling. (Comperatore and Nerone 2008)

This is distinctly reflected in their consumer behavior. **Millennials famously look for authenticity from brands and businesses.** They don't settle for corporate promises; they want to see action. (Wylonis 2021) Why? Because it's very important to Millennials that they patronize a business whose values align with their own, especially when it comes to diversity and the environment. To a millennial, what a brand does out in the world is just as important as the product it produces. In fact, research has shown that roughly half of millennials (52 percent) wanted retailers to align with their values. Compare that to only 35 percent of the previous generation (the baby boomers). (Sterling 2018). An overwhelming 85 percent of Millennials also expressed that they liked the idea of retailers supporting charities.

As Millennials lead the push for more corporate authenticity, **all consumers have come to enjoy the benefits of the resulting expressions of generosity and benevolence.** A company that markets with an intention behind them, a value system, and a commitment to making the world a better place captures all of our attentions. We believe, we admire, and ultimately, we support.

WAYS TO MARKET WITH INTENTION

If you are in business, you are always marketing, in everything you do, make, and post. In fact, one of the ways you may be marketing unintentionally is through your corporate social responsibility (CSR).

A company's CSR sends a message to

consumers: **This is what we stand for. Are you with us?** It's a powerful way to get consumers on board with a brand or product. It allows them to raise their hands and join a movement. And who doesn't want to feel included and good about the company they keep?

Between 2011-2018, the amount of S&P 500 companies that published sustainability or CSR reports rose 66 percent! (wbdynamics.com n.d.) The continued rise in CSR among companies, big and small, is no coincidence. Companies have come to realize that when it comes to attracting business, especially from millennials, they need to express their corporate values in the world.

If we look at some of the most high-ranking brands among millennials, we'll find some of the big names—Amazon and Google. (Comparably 2021) If we look a little deeper, we'll see why the millennials are attracted to these brands that cater to their needs and share their passions.

AMAZON

When he started Amazon in 1994, Jeff Bezos had a keen eye on how his target market would develop. He was convinced that if he could keep competitors focused on Amazon while Amazon stayed focus on the customer, they would win. (Business Insider 2018) And they have. Today, about 60 percent of millennial consumers cite Amazon as their preferred shopping channel. It even beats Google as the place to start their online shopping searches and research for planned purchases. (Danziger 2021)

Amazon courted the millennial market by tailoring products to them. Personalization is important to this audience, with 88 percent of millennials valuing it in the brands they patronize. (Danziger 2021) Millennials appreciate Amazon's personal suggestions for products, fueled by algorithms. They applaud Amazon Smile, which gives customers the option to donate a percentage of their purchase to their favorite charity. As college students, millennials benefit from the student rates available for Amazon Prime subscriptions. **Most importantly, they recognize and value the transparency of Amazon and their commitment to greater causes, like climate change.** Right on their website, Amazon expresses commitment to net-zero carbon by 2040 and is working towards reducing water usage in data centers, using sustainable aviation fuel, and ensuring that partners in their supply chain are treated with fundamental dignity and respect. Amazon also is striving towards gender inequity by supporting the United Nation's Women's Empowerment Principles. In 2021 they made a $1 million donation to the Resilience Fund for Women in Global Value Chains. (Amazon 2021) Clearly, Amazon is transparent about what it is doing and how all its customers, especially concerned millennials, understand their commitment to CSR.

GOOGLE

Likewise, Google demonstrated its transparency by pioneering the epitome of user-generated content—the Google review. Today, a reported 97 percent of millennials read online reviews before selecting a business. (Fertik 2019) However, it's also Google's CSR that has earned it a reputation among millennials as a cool place to work. In 2019, Google achieved thirteen consecutive years of carbon neutrality. It was able to match 100 percent of its annual electricity usage with renewable energy, making it the world's largest annual corporate purchaser of renewable energy (CSR Journal 2021). Google did it through designing efficient data centers, which provided job creation, economic development, educational programs, and environmental and cultural projects. It also reduced waste by effectively using refurbished parts for their machine upgrades and recycling machinery it no longer uses. All of it goes to waste-to-energy facilities and other sustainable pathways. (CSR Journal 2021) IT also is trying to utilize water more efficiently and harness wind and solar energy. It has declared that by 2030, it will run its business on carbon-free energy throughout the world.

Conservation also is important to Google. Its campuses are built with respect for the environment and science-based Habitat Design Guidelines. For example, Google has a thriving egret rookery in the middle of its Mountain View, California, campus. (CSR Journal 2021)

Google's products also express its eco-friendly corporate values. For example, the Nest Thermostat has saved over 50 billion kWh of energy since its introduction. The innovation can save the average customer 3-5 percent on their home's heating and cooling systems. (CSR Journal 2021) With millennials being always open to the next best thing, they also are keeping an eye on Google's work towards a self-driving car and how that will facilitate car-sharing and ultimately, fewer cars on the road, and cleaner air. (D'Allegro 2022)

These are just some examples of two brands that are universally loved by millennials and how the company's values align with their own. The message is clear. Consumers are paying attention to what businesses are doing. If you have not been transparent with your customers about your CSR, now is the time. If you don't have CSR in place, now is the time to consider it.

CSR is just one important way to market in the 21st century. Here are some more ways to show your audience that your company is more than a good product.

STORYTELLING

Everyone tells stories, including brands. Storytelling is a series of facts, couched in an emotional narrative that speaks to our souls to fulfill a primal need.

From our childhood days sitting on our mother's lap, our brains have been conditioned to like and appreciate stories. It's also easier to remember lessons from stories, which is why famous storytellers from Jesus Christ to Aesop chose the medium to teach others.

Smart marketers in the 21st century will bring storytelling into their content in every way possible. For example:

CASE STUDIES

Take the problem-solution-result formula for an average case study and fashion it into something more memorable to the reader. Look at the two examples below. Which do you find more memorable? More fun to read?

CASE STUDY #1:

A CEO needed help launching a product by the end of the year. They hired us to develop a marketing plan, including a targeted marketing campaign and a press release in the media. We successfully launched on December 1 and sold 1,000 units by the end of the year.

CASE STUDY #2:

The CEO was speeding towards the lowest fourth quarter (Q4) earnings in ten years unless something could be done. He had a great idea that he knew would work, but only if he could launch the product in the next three months. He didn't think it was possible until he called us. With our proven, systematic plan, we crafted a targeted marketing campaign and worked late into the night and early in the morning with our eyes on the deadline— December 1. When our press release and campaign hit the media, his website was on fire with orders—more than 1,000 in the first month. Q4 was saved and the New Year promised amazing revenue!

Note how the second version uses some elements of storytelling, and a narrative arc. We start with an inciting incident (headed towards the lowest Q4 earnings in ten years) and follow with rising action (the call to the agency), the falling action (the work towards the conclusion) and the resolution. Note how we used language and detail to draw us into the emotion of the situation from the first sentence. Creative storytelling is more fun to read and will help customers remember what you did!

PUBLIC RELATIONS

Sometimes, the press release, isn't just an announcement of a new product or a new CEO. It also can be a storytelling element about your business. Have you retooled a process to see amazing growth? Are you responding to world current events in a unique way? Have you found a unique way to serve your audience that your competitors have not? Is there someone at your company who is making headlines and is an unsung hero that you'd like to sing about? These are all stories that can be pitched to the right reporter at the right publication or website. Who knows where the right story can lead?

THE VISUAL

Storytelling doesn't necessarily have to be a written. You can use video to tell your story. Or take an arresting photograph. Draw a satirical cartoon. Create an infographic-style flowchart to tell the story of your process. Be creative in how you tell your story and market your brand. Your audience will thank you for it.

YOUR BRAND ARCHETYPE

A brand archetype is the "character" your company plays within your customer's story. Embracing a brand archetype shows an understanding of the customer and what they want. Everyone has a preferred archetype for their own personal story, and some of the best ones are those we identify with. Knowing your customer and which archetype will appeal to them most will help you choose yours.

When you think about brand archetypes, think of your company as not just selling a product but taking on a role in the lives of your customers. Then ask, what role are you fulfilling in your customers' lives? For example, you might be there to save the day, like Superman. Lean into that narrative when you write your case studies. Other quintessential brand archetypes and their brands include "the rebel" (embodied by the

What special role do you play in the lives of your clients that you can assume as your brand archetype?

Harley Davison brand), "the magician" (embodied by Disney), and "the explorer" (embodied by Patagonia). What special role do you play in the lives of your clients that you can assume as your brand archetype? Address it in your marketing and your corporate values.

THE HUMAN TOUCH

When the pandemic hit, we all retreated to our home offices to work virtually. When we did, something ironic happened. We removed ourselves from daily, in-person contact, but we unintentionally got more personal by sharing our at-home spaces with colleagues. Online meetings bring people into our homes, where we are sometimes interrupted by our small children and pets. On occasion, we may catch a glimpse of the posters on someone's wall (who knew they were a Grateful Dead fan?), a golf trophy, photographs, or something else very personal. It tells us something about the person we did not know and probably wouldn't have known otherwise. And when we can learn a little bit more about someone's personal life, it makes us feel more connected to them. It gives us a chance to feel something in common with them and understand their worldview.

It's the same with your brand and your audience. **The more you can offer the human touch, the more they will get to know you, feel connected, and be more friendly to your brand.** Video is a great medium for this. Show your customers what happens behind the scenes. The making of your product. A day in the life of your CEO. Explore and capture how real people interact with your product. You may be surprised at what your audience likes and shares.

CONGRUENCY

When you are marketing with intention, it means that everything you do and stand for is consistent and predictable. Audiences today have little patience for hypocritical brands. If a company or brand says they stand for something or that they are going to do something, they better do it!

The same attitude extends to people and celebrities. Will Smith shocked the world when he slapped Chris Rock at the Oscars for making an inappropriate remark about his wife. We all knew Will Smith as an even-tempered, amiable man until that moment. His behavior was incongruent with his image. We are similarly appalled when someone we have come to know and trust as a decent person, like Prince Andrew or Bill Cosby, is suddenly linked to a scandalous association or accusation. **Again, the incongruency makes us feel tricked and foolish that the person we thought we knew was actually someone different.** It's a lesson to us as marketers to always be real in the image we portray to the public. They deserve our honesty, or we will suffer their backlash if our hypocrisy is uncovered.

YOUR CRISIS COMMUNICATION

When a crisis hits, the spotlight falls hard upon a company and its leadership. Their next move can make or break them.

If a company has been marketing with intention all along and has established a congruent image among its audiences, **their response to the crisis should be more straightforward.** The response should align with the company's core values and their audiences' expectations. If it does not, the company will be judged harshly.

Companies in crisis must handle their response with grace. The world will be closely watching everything—their company website, all social media, the network news, and homemade videos by people in the vicinity—to see how the company responds. And that response will elicit a positive or negative feeling from their audience. Those feelings might be compassion or empathy, or outrage or disappointment based on how authentic the company response is. For example, if the company claims to be environmentally-friendly but the crisis harms the environment, the company must quickly respond to make amends to the earth or face the criticism of their customers. Every action counts when a company is responding to a crisis.

The idea of crisis communication may not feel like part of a company's marketing plan, but in actuality, it is. Every company should have a crisis communication plan well in advance. So, when the time comes, the company may respond with grace, and in alignment with its values.

MARKETING WITH INTENTION WITH THE GOLDEN FIVE

Marketing with intention is important to reach today's sophisticated audiences. It's done in a variety of ways and should be the foundational goal of your company and/or brand's marketing. The five types of marketing described in Part II of this book are underscored by the intention. Each of the five types can help a company fulfill its mission to express its core values in everything it does.

How a company tactically carries out its mission depends on several things. Perhaps, however, one of the most important things is the way in which a company does it. In other words, the marketing vehicles it chooses.

The idea of crisis communication may not feel like part of a company's marketing plan, but in actuality, it is.

CHAPTER 3

SELECTING MARKETING VEHICLES

Marketing is a lot like life. There's no "one way" to do it right.

Let's take the simple example of going to the store. If you live in the city, you might think about walking, or maybe taking public transportation, or riding a bicycle. If you live in the suburbs, you probably will need a car. Then you have to factor in your preferences. I'm a pilot, so if I can fly there in my sport plane, that's my preferred method—if the weather cooperates. Other people may look in their garage and have the choice between a practical, roomy SUV or a vintage convertible sportscar. Which one would you take for a drive with the whole family? How about a night on the town? There are important reasons behind our choices in life, and there are equally important reasons behind choosing our marketing vehicles to carry out a strategy.

Marketing 101 tells us the three main components to marketing: audience, message, and vehicles. In other words, marketing is directed by who we want to reach, what we want to say, and how we want to say it. Of the three main components, the marketing vehicles—those ways that we choose to spread our message—can sometimes be the hardest to plan. The considerations are many, and when you're trailblazing, you may not have any statistics or precedence to help you make decisions. You just may have to go with your gut, which can always be a gamble that could have you end up winning big or losing everything.

MARKETING VEHICLES

As I work with clients, I see varying amounts of information that clients know and don't know about the marketing vehicles available to them. Some are more informed than others. However, we want to educate all of our clients!

To bridge the knowledge gap, I was inspired to produce a special giveaway to explain the many marketing vehicles available to them, and their unique selling points. It's a set of playing cards called "The Marketing Deliverable Mix." This fun, brightly colored, iconized, easy to hold and sort deck of cards informs clients and prospects about the many ways they can reach their audience with their messages. The deck was developed to inspire clients to look at new and different marketing vehicles to incorporate into their marketing strategies.

Although the deck is still very helpful, it could potentially contain several more cards. That's because marketing strategies grow and change very quickly, fueled by technology and apps. Below is a list of marketing vehicles that I've assembled as a menu of options for anybody looking for a comprehensive marketing strategy. I include a description and also my own personal assessment of the cost versus the effectiveness of using that vehicle. Both of them are rated out of five dollar signs and stars.

EMAILS

Emails have become an excellent strategy for marketing events, downloadable assets, and sharing online resources and links. We consider

Marketing is a lot like life. There's no "one way" to do it right.

a good open rate for clients to be anything above 8 percent, with the more important statistic of clickthrough rate being at least 2 percent, which is the national average. (hubspot.com 2022) The pros of emails include the ability to target and personalize. The cons include the competition. Most people get plenty of messages in their inbox and yours is liable to be missed. Email is best tracked when there is a specific call to action, such as a request to register for an event or download a content piece.

Cost: $ Effectiveness: **

WORD OF MOUTH

Word of mouth is, was, and always will be your very best form of advertising. Word-of-mouth marketing includes referral programs, online reviews, and informal conversations with existing clients to gain leads and presentations where you share valuable information. Pros include the personal relationship that can develop when people actually meet you. The cons? Motivating shy people to sing your praises, especially with an online review. The millennials and Generation Z are specifically conscious of online reviews and in fact, 91 percent say they trust online reviews as much as personal recommendations. Of all American consumers, 93 percent say that online reviews influenced their purchase decisions. (Kaemingk 2020)

Cost: Free Effectiveness: *****

DISPLAY ADVERTISING

Traditional advertising remains a popular way to market messages. In fact, in 2020, 33 percent of marketers used paid advertising to increase their awareness. (hubspot.com 2022) Website banners, social media paid campaigns, billboards, and inserts are all unrequested forms of communication from your audience, but they still have a place in the marketing mix. One of the cons to advertising is the price of space or air time; television, radio, and online ad space (although less expensive) still requires a sizeable investment.

Tracking true ROI typically requires an extra step like utilizing a "fake" contact phone number or providing a quick response (QR) code to a specific landing page. Campaigns should be done no less than ninety consecutive days to assess effectiveness. **Cost: $$$$ Effectiveness: *****

SOCIAL MEDIA

Social media marketing can be an effective tool if used on the right platform with the right message. Every platform requires a specific tone and audience. The frequency of your activity should depend upon the platform you are targeting as well. Instagram (83 percent) now surpasses Facebook (80 percent) and Twitter (62 percent) as the top social media platform for businesses. (hubspot.com 2022) The pros of social media include its affordability—it's free except for the creative and administrative help needed to create consistent posts. The cons include the content creation side, and the ongoing energy it takes to produce a steady stream of posts, and to monitor what's posted to reply to comments.

Cost: $ Effectiveness: ***

STRATEGIC ALLIANCES

This refers to marketing in which you connect with another business or individual for an effective collaboration of your services. Your expectation for these alliances will vary, depending on the length of and specifics of your arrangement. Some examples include offering your service or expertise in conjunction with someone else, partnering with a non-profit to create a "feel good" story or experience, or collaborating with an organization to promote an event. These kinds of alliances can lead to a big boost in business, although some entrepreneurs who work better solo may have trouble compromising or meeting the expectations of their strategic partners.

Cost: Free - Effectiveness: *****

CONTENT MARKETING

This type of marketing uses storytelling and information to provide a piece of valuable written content to prospective clients that will guide them to a specific course of action. This would include downloadable content pieces and eBooks, blogs, and website content. The content typically has a trackable call to action that may entice people onto a website or landing page, where they can place an order or share a piece of content on their own social media. Because you are creating content for the audience to find, their response to it, if found, is usually quite good. Pros include the shareability of each online asset, the relatively low production cost, and the ease of tracking ROI with analytic software. Cons include having to market each piece of content so it gets found in the first place.

Cost: $$ Effectiveness: ***

PUBLIC RELATIONS

This form of marketing involves conveying a newsworthy story or area of expertise to the media to feature in their news outlet. Examples would be press releases, media alerts, fact sheets, story angle sheets, etc. Your hope is to get unpaid, third-party endorsement of your story as share worthy (at no charge), as opposed to advertising, which is paid placement. Your cost is in the distribution, and media have the final say whether or not they will use their news. However, nationally distributed news releases typically yield scores of new shares, which help with client search engine optimization (SEO). When done right, you can even become a source for the media to quote.

Cost: $$$ Effectiveness: ****

SEARCH ENGINE MARKETING (SEM)

Using the power of search engines (like Google) to spread ad campaigns can land your ad squarely in the eyeline of consumers who need your products most—at the top of the page of the search results. It's a quick way to get to the number one spot on Google. This type of marketing requires monitoring, and sometimes changing up your keywords to stay effective. A big pro is that you can set the budget (which must be considerable to see traction) to spend on each campaign. The biggest con is the cost, yet this type of marketing can be very effective in a short period of time.

Cost: \$\$\$\$\$ Effectiveness: ****

SEARCH ENGINE OPTIMIZATION (SEO)

Most marketers understand the concept of Google keywords and how using them in headlines and in strategic places on the website (such as the title tag and page meta data) can lift a company in their search engine results page (SERP). While SEM is a pay-to-play strategy, SEO is a close cousin of SEM that is much more affordable. In 2021, 71 percent of marketers said using strategic keywords was their number one strategy for SEO. (hubspot.com 2022) SEO can be quite effective in getting your products and services in front of people that want them, even though it may take some time. Also, it might take a consultant or a dedicated person to help you properly target your keywords and keep you abreast of the constantly changing algorithms in the search engines so your SEO strategy stays fresh.

Cost: \$\$ Effectiveness: ****

THOUGHT LEADERSHIP

A thought leader is someone who is a sought-after subject matter expert. If people know you are the expert, they will come to you. Thought leaders typically make their expertise known through releasing online content, writing a book, making media appearances, or holding workshops. The pros of being a thought leader is that once you reach thought leader status, your name automatically markets you! The con is the hard work involved to get to the top of the heap.

A marketing company can show you the shortcuts, but the work and commitment you need is real. You have to stand out and provide value.

Cost: $$$ Effectiveness: **

MARKETING COLLATERAL

Most companies have a logo, a brochure, perhaps a business card, and (although it may be online these days) some sort of letterhead. Print pieces still make an impact as a mailer or handout in meetings or at trade shows. Your marketing collateral screams, "I'm a serious, established business." In the digital world, the tactile, physically present brochure still has clout. For example, brochures delivered through door-drop marketing can stay in a house for thirty-eight days, and 23 percent of them get circulated to family members or friends. And 61 percent of people buy products once they see them in brochures. (Brown 2021) Thus, the old-fashioned marketing collateral, once the staple of every business, still has value.

Cost: $ Effectiveness: $$$

VIDEO MARKETING

Video has exploded over the past decade. More video platforms like TikTok have emerged, and thanks to technology, videos have become easier for amateurs to produce. In 2020, a survey found that people watch an average of nineteen hours of online video per week, and 88 percent of them say they've been convinced to buy a product or service by watching a brand's video. (Melvin 2022) Videos can be as simple as a greeting or quick explainer or a more sophisticated, professionally produced, scripted and voice-overed short movie. Budget is always an issue with video marketing but know that well-done videos can be extremely effective.

Cost: $-$$$$$ Effectiveness: **

GUERILLA MARKETING

Just as aggressive and focused as it sounds, guerilla marketing is carried out by targeting one segment in a very specific, grassroots way. It could be attending an event to meet a certain person or blanketing the window shields of cars in a particular parking lot with a flyer. It could be a protest, a boycott, a flash mob, or a strategically-placed editorial. It's done for a specific reason in a specific place and typically in a unique or unexpected way. It works great when instituted over time, and when you need to establish a direct connection to a certain audience and the opportunity arises to make that connection.

Cost: $ Effectiveness: ****

EVENT MARKETING

From conferences to book launches, to open houses, ribbon cuttings, cocktail parties, and webinars, when you gather people to learn, celebrate, or promote something, magic can happen. Since these opportunities are typically "opt in," they can be very effective with a smaller, focused audience. The trick is getting busy people to attend. If it's an in-person event, you now have the added challenge of getting people out of their house since people have become accustomed to virtual events during the pandemic. As for planning the events themselves, some of the trends we're seeing are the need for personalized marketing, offering hybrid events, and keeping health and safety as a top priority for in-person gatherings. (Fourneau 2022)

Cost: $$$$ Effectiveness: ***

TRADE SHOWS

The marketing vehicle that was the first to be completely decimated by the pandemic has come roaring back. In 2022, 85 percent of trade show marketers surveyed expected their attendance to return to pre-pandemic level attendance. (Pofeldt 2022) Trade shows provide a powerful venue to meet and greet prospects, make the most of existing marketing assets (like videos and brochures), and also provide demonstrations or other experiential marketing opportunities. Attending trade shows is a big investment in creating an exhibit and human resources to man the booth but if the right audience is there, great connections can be made!

Cost: $$$$$ Effectiveness: *

SPONSORSHIPS

Another great way to increase awareness for your brand is to sponsor an event or part of an event in the community or at a trade show. In the community this could mean a festival or fair, or sporting events or concerts. At a trade show this would mean sponsoring a breakfast, cocktail party, networking event or a speaker. The top five most effective types of sponsorship opportunities, as ranked by the survey participants, were speaking opportunities, networking events, social media, show-eblasts and show boards/graphics. (Stanton 2019)

Cost: $$$$$ Effectiveness: *

DIRECT MAIL

Despite the proliferation of digital marketing, direct mail is alive and well and being used by lots of companies to deliver their marketing messages. Where it's a struggle to keep up with our digital inboxes, some experts, including me, think direct mail is swinging back into fashion. Recent studies show that 42.2 percent of direct mail recipients either read or scan the mail they get, and direct mail offers a 29 percent return on investment. (V. 2022) It is somewhat of a novelty now, and well-done advertisements can actually stand out splendidly in the regular mailbox. The drawback is the cost; printing is expensive, even for marketing programs that send your direct mail or coupon in a pack with others.

Cost: $$$$ Effectiveness: $$$

EXPERIENTIAL MARKETING

When a brand provides a sample, or a simulated situation to help people experience their product or service, we call it experiential marketing. This type of marketing takes creativity, and a way to showcase the experiential marketing experience. They involve giving people a chance to immerse themselves in the use of the product, much like the "free makeovers" offered at department stores; a virtual developer letting people use virtual reality (VR) goggles at a trade show; or even sending a free sample of perfume or food in the mail. Experiential marketing ensnares multiple senses and allows people to interact intimately with a product or service. It can make a product or service downright irresistible! As technology progresses, I would imagine experiential marketing will become accessible for any company that wants to use it.

Cost: $$$$ Effectiveness: ***

AUDIO BROADCASTS AND PODCASTS

Podcasts are popular and increasing in popularity as I write this! Ad revenues for podcasts are expected to exceed $2 billion in 2023, fueled by an American population where almost 60 percent of US consumers listen to podcasts. Of weekly listeners, they average eight podcasts per week. (Molenaar 2022) Podcasts are a marketing vehicle of choice for content creators and thought leaders who want to be known as experts on a certain subject. However, it is interesting to note that as popular as podcasts are, AM/FM radio is still found to outperform podcasts in the car. In 2020, 91 percent of people tuned into their radio station rather than a podcast. (Molenaar 2022) Podcasts may be difficult to launch and maintain but they are great marketing vehicles when your subject matter has depth and requires explanation. Be sure to always have a call to action at the end of your podcast, in your show notes, etc. to link your podcast back to your website.

Cost: $$$ Effectiveness: $$$

EMERGING MARKETING VEHICLES

As mentioned before, marketing changes with the world. When the pandemic hit, we needed to pivot the marketing for many of our clients at JJR. The marketing vehicles that had worked so well for us in the past (such as in-person events) required a reschedule or a reimagination. Sometimes it was as easy as moving the event online, like our book launches that were very timely events. However, for our brick-and-mortar customers, their clientele no longer headed through their doors. We needed to help them strategize differently. The coronavirus shutdown led us to employ more non-traditional marketing vehicles in service to our clients. Some of these vehicles were already on the rise, enjoying a healthy market share. Others were illuminated by the pandemic. There are four in particular that we see as "emerging." They are increasing in popularity because they fulfill a special niche for many.

INFLUENCER MARKETING

In a sense, influencer marketing is nothing new. For years, companies have paid celebrities to be their spokespeople for certain causes or products. Television advertisers have used celebrity spokespeople for years (think Taylor Swift for Diet Coke or Sally Struthers for Save the Children Federation). But in the world of influencer marketing, relationship is what rules, not necessarily celebrity. That's because you may never personally speak with Taylor or Sally, but by following someone's social media profile, you have the potential to personally interact with that celebrity influencer. And that's very exciting.

The influencer marketing industry has grown dramatically from $1.7 billion in 2016 to $16.4 billion expected in 2022! (Santora 2022) Who are these influencers generating this revenue? They are typically, but not always, internet-famous individuals on a particular social media platform like YouTube or Instagram. Influencers typically have thousands, if not millions of followers and/

or subscribers. Influencer marketing is especially helpful with consumer products. Product samples are introduced to the influencer so that they, in turn, can introduce them to their followers. A marketing company can help hook you up with influencers, but the marketing magic comes from the relationships that the influencer has developed between themselves and their followers. Followers believe influencers because of their relationship with the influencer. This is a very effective strategy. But the difficult part, depending on your product or service, is finding an influencer willing to represent your brand who feels comfortable doing so. Influencers know their followers are looking for them to be authentic so they can only give honest endorsements of products. If not, they will end up dealing with negative feedback and even a loss of their lovingly cultivated audience members.

Cost: $$$$ Effectiveness: **

ECOMMERCE SUBSCRIPTION SERVICES

With an ecommerce subscription, people receive a product and/or service through the mail on a regular basis and pay a fee for it. There are three types of ecommerce subscriptions services. Curation subscriptions are the most popular, accounting for about 55 percent of subscribers. (Chen, et al. 2018) In curation subscriptions, the subscriber receives a product and/or service every month. For example, StitchFix sends subscribers new outfits in the mail and Birchbox shares a box of sample beauty products.

Replenishment subscriptions account for about 32 percent of subscriptions (Chen, et al. 2018) and provide a replacement (typically in the mail) for something you regularly consume. An example would be the Dollar Shave Club that delivers new razors every month and HelloFresh that provides meal kits.

The remaining 13 percent of subscribers have "access" subscriptions (Chen, et al. 2018) that offer the ability to view or use content, a service, or a software. This would apply to companies like Netflix, which delivers videos, Peapod Digital Labs for grocery shopping, or Mailchimp for an online marketing platform. For a company with a new or very niche product, becoming an "ingredient" in one of the subscription boxes sent to consumers can be a great way to reach a new targeted audience. Incidentally, while you would think that convenience would be the main reason someone would sign up for a subscription, it often isn't. In a survey asking people why they signed up for subscription services, their top three answers were good value for the price, high quality, and a good variety of items or experiences. (McKinsey & Company 2021) Subscribers like variety, so maybe your product would bring a breath of fresh air to the typical subscription.

Cost: $$ Effectiveness: **

CROWDSOURCING

When an entrepreneur wants to get a project off the ground, crowdsourcing is a great way to begin assembling financial support, and ultimately, a tribe of ambassadors. With crowdsourcing you actively seek funders for your project online on sites like Kickstarter and Indiegogo. People can share their dreams with others and then watch them come true as people pledge funds in order to be in on the ground floor of something special. Best of all, as you receive financial backing through the platform, you will be marketing your project through your followers. When the project is complete, you have a mini-marketing force all set to order and share the product.

Crowdfunding is a successful strategy. More than $17.2 billion is generated annually through crowdfunding in North America. (Shepherd 2020) However, the contributions may not be tax free, so check the specifics of your desired site and confer with your accountant to see if it is the most efficient approach for you. Also, you have to know your audience. People between the ages of twenty-four and thirty-five are more likely to participate in a crowdfunding campaign than someone over forty-five years of age. (Shepherd 2020)

Cost: $$$$$ Effectiveness: ***

SELF-PUBLISHING

I don't know who said it first, but "books are the new business card." In our publishing house, Fig Factor Media, we have had many authors come to us wanting a book to give them credibility as a subject matter expert. In many cases, these emerging authors already had speaking engagements, and were being asked the question, "Where's your book?" Now that self-publishing is an available and respected way to create and share content, experts don't have much of an excuse not to tell their story. Books not only lead to notoriety but can lead to speaking engagements and a whole host of other opportunities.

Cost: $$$ Effectiveness: ***

EMERGING AUDIENCE CONSIDERATIONS

When you consider all the marketing vehicles available, it's no wonder it's so important to have a specific strategy so you can chart your best course. It also doesn't hurt to have the expert guidance of a marketing team.

Remember that your audience and their particular interests and needs should be the main directive for selecting your marketing vehicles. Also, as we market in the 21st century, there are a few things that are considered universally important to most audiences:

ESG

Environmental, social, and governance (ESG) refers to the company's concern for the planet, social justice, and its awareness of laws that may be undermining its audience's specific concerns. For example, be aware of your audience's sensitivity to the environmental issues, like climate change and reducing waste, because they are watching your company to see how you respond authentically to their concerns. For some companies, this means the end of using print marketing materials to show their sincerity to the cause. For others, it means mentioning and promoting the company's stellar sustainability efforts as a specific tentacle of their marketing strategy. One study revealed we are still learning in this area. While 90 percent of executives find sustainability to be important, only 60 percent have sustainability incorporated into their business model. (Haanaes 2022) Your audience is looking for your authentic response to the ESG issues they care about most. How will your company reply?

DIVERSITY

Audiences, especially members of the Millennial and Gen Z, are very aware of diversity, equity and inclusion (DEI) in the corporate setting. They want to work with and support businesses that welcome the differences between us in the workforce. That includes race, gender, ethnicity, religious affiliation, national origin, sexual orientation, disability, and age. According to one study, more than 75 percent of job applicants report that having a diverse workforce is important when making a decision on where to work, yet only 40 percent of organizations have mature diversity initiatives. (Beasley 2021) In terms of marketing, be aware of your audience's sensitivities to DEI and be sure to make your marketing messages appropriate and inclusive to all audiences. In your marketing messages, choose inclusive visual imagery, too. A diversity-focused marketing company can help with this, as can an in-house DEI department with a shared interest in promoting diversity within your company.

HEALTH AND WELLNESS

As our world becomes more complex, so does our ability as a human race to deal with it. Mental illness is on the rise in America, with 50 million Americans (19.86 percent of adults) reporting that they have experienced a mental illness. (Mental Health America 2022) Depression, anxiety, and suicidal ideation are, unfortunately, also more prevalent in young people. **For marketers, this means that we must be in touch with the health and mental wellness benefits of our unique product and service.** This way, we can deliver to our audience not only what they are looking for, but what is good for them as well.

MARKETING VEHICLES AND THE GOLDEN FIVE FRAMEWORK

One way of looking at marketing in the 21st century is through an examination of the ways we market, as we did in this chapter. Another way to do it is functionally, through the lens of the Golden Five types of marketing that will encompass these vehicles, as well as your marketing intention and the challenges that exist in marketing today. We're now ready to dive into the treasure chest within the Golden Five Framework and see what they will mean for your marketing. Ready? Let's go!

PART TWO

THE GOLDEN FIVE FRAMEWORK

CHAPTER 4

FOUNDATIONAL MARKETING

During the COVID-19 shelter-in-place order in Chicago, my nonprofit client was approached by a sign company with an idea. The sign company wanted to produce a sign honoring first responders with the name of the nonprofit on it. Not only would the yard signs serve to bolster the morale of the first responders, but it also could create a fundraising revenue stream for the nonprofit.

My client immediately said, "Yes." The printing company designed the signs and sent a sample to her. Delighted beyond all expectation with the result, she eagerly took a photo of it displayed on a lawn and produced a compelling Instagram post encouraging everyone to buy a sign and support her cause.

There were only a few things wrong with what she did.

She didn't have the agreement ironed out with the printer as to the cost of each sign and how quickly they could be printed and delivered. She also didn't have an order mechanism set up on her website. She hadn't thought about how many signs she would need total. And when people started calling to order the signs, she had nowhere to send them.

What was the misstep? She didn't have the first kind of marketing in place that is needed for any marketing effort: foundational marketing.

WHAT IS FOUNDATIONAL MARKETING?

As the name suggests, your foundational marketing is the body of marketing mechanisms you *absolutely need in place* for your company's marketing efforts or your campaign to succeed. Your foundational elements create the baseline of your marketing activity.

Everyone needs foundational marketing. Foundational efforts introduce you to your prospective clientele in online and offline ways, and it is exceptionally critical for newer and start-up businesses. After all, when you are starting a venture from scratch with no marketing whatsoever, it makes sense to get busy creating an online and offline presence, so the public knows you are in business.

However, as you can see from our story about the yard sign, it's easy for even the most seasoned entrepreneurs to skip the critical step of getting their foundational marketing in order before they begin promoting. Enthusiasm and urgency can propel you ahead to places you are unprepared and unequipped to go.

Let's delve a little deeper into the pieces of the foundational marketing puzzle you will undoubtedly need for your efforts. Build them and then blend them for best results.

> It's important for every company to clearly understand who they are and why they are in business.

61

Even established companies may feel the need to "rebrand" at some point in their lifecycle.

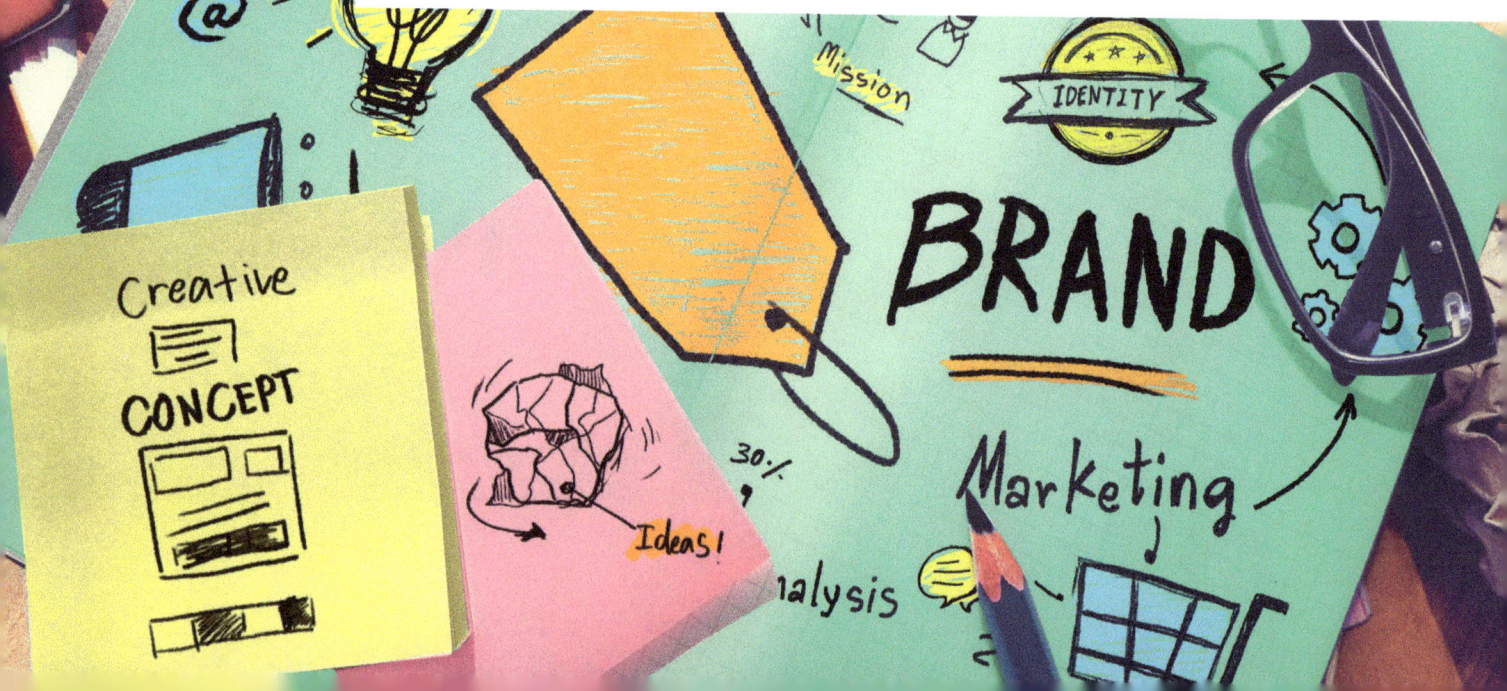

CORPORATE BRANDING

Who am I? It's an age-old question we ask ourselves as individuals, right? But business entities need to ask themselves the same thing, especially as they launch themselves into the world. **It's important for every company to clearly understand who they are and why they are in business.** Likewise, it's important for customers to know who a company is and what's behind them. It's like having a glimpse into a company's soul.

In my extensive work consulting with start-up companies, as well as launching my own businesses and nonprofits, I have found that marketing a company well begins with the creation of their corporate branding. This is a necessary step that should be done before work on any marketing materials (including a website) should begin. If this step is skipped, the effects show up further down the road. Confusion ensues and questions reign supreme. What should we write? How should we describe ourselves? If the corporate branding element is already well-considered and in place, much of the work is done already!

Even established companies may feel the need to "rebrand" at some point in their lifecycle. The right rebrand can be amazingly successful. For example, the rebrand of Dunkin' Donuts to Dunkin' came with a fresh look, a bevy of newly introduced menu changes to appeal to younger audiences, and trendy "merch" with their truncated, yet livelier new logo. The company also successfully courted the youth market by forging a successful partnership with TikTok star Charli D'Amelio, who helped them create a signature drink, "The Charli." (Meisenzahl 2021)

Regardless of whether you're doing your corporate branding exercise as a new business or a rebrand, consider the following elements before you dive into your new or revised marketing efforts. It may mean setting aside time with key players in the company and/or trusted advisors to make sure the optimal decisions are made. Discuss and decide the following, and make sure you commit it to paper!

YOUR COMPANY'S NAME

First things first. A new company needs a new name. In most cases, it makes sense to define your company through its corporate branding elements before you make the final decision on a name. That way if you are going for a playful vibe, you can come up with a more playful name. Similarly, if you're rebranding, a name change may or may not be necessary. Sometimes it is and sometimes it isn't, depending again on your target market, competition, and overall branding strategy. It certainly worked for Dunkin' (formerly Dunkin' Donuts) and KFC (formerly Kentucky Fried Chicken).

YOUR COMPANY'S MISSION

Your mission is not only what services you offer and to whom, but it also looks beyond the profit. What kind of impact do you want to have on your community? On the world? If you are rebranding, is there a new audience you are trying to reach? Make it part of your mission.

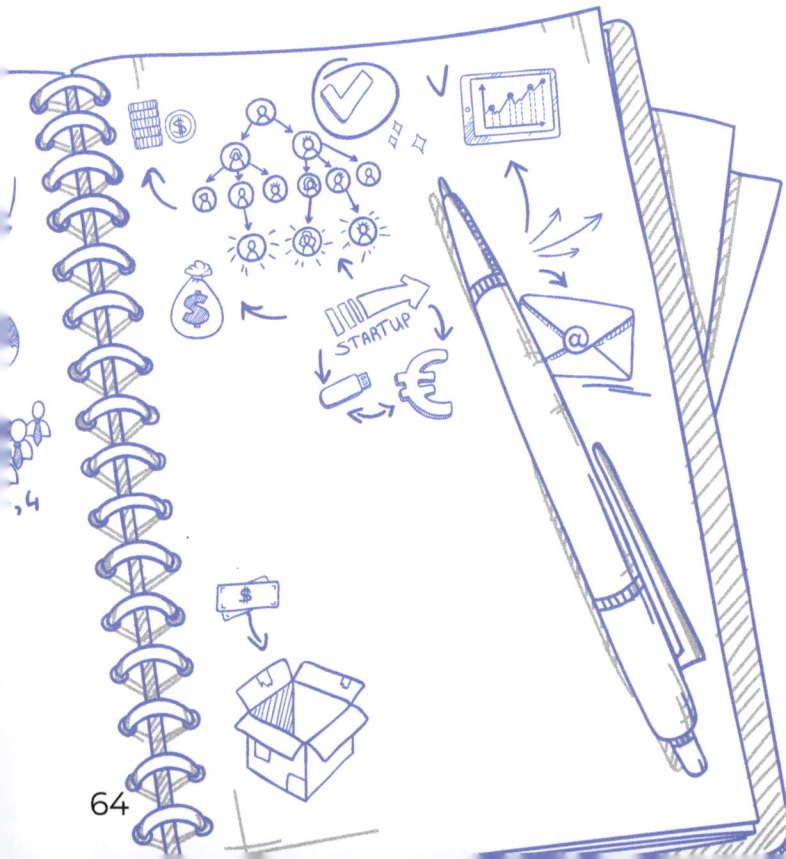

YOUR COMPANY'S VISION

This is not some pie-in-the-sky, catchy motto to impress your customers. Rather, it is a truly thought-out, challenging, but attainable goal that your company can achieve with enough success. The unspoken idea is that if your customers want to help you achieve the vision, they will support you.

YOUR COMPANY'S VALUES

Your company's values will guide you in making all kinds of decisions in line with your company mission and vision. Once you've determined and digested your company's values, you'll understand how you should conduct business to demonstrate your commitment to them. Today's consumers have their eye out for a company's corporate social responsibility (CSR). In fact, up to 91 percent of millennials and 90 percent of Generation Z consumers report being more willing to purchase products with a social or environmental benefit. (Sourcing Journal 2019)

YOUR COMPANY'S STORY

The origin story of your company also can be a powerful marketing tool. Through the art of storytelling, you can unfold your founder's story and their true motivation for being in business. These stories are typically intriguing and relatable, and often align with the values of the prospective customers. Some agencies that have aimed to inspire and motivate their readers through storytelling have seen a 20-30 percent increase in brand engagement. (Forbes Agency Council 2020) Customers who relate to your story become endeared to your brand.

YOUR COMPANY'S UNIQUE SELLING PROPOSITIONS (USPS)

Most entrepreneurs open a company because they detect an unmet need in the marketplace. How will your company differ from your competitors? The answer to this question leads to your unique selling proposition and should be crystal clear before you begin your marketing efforts.

YOUR COMPANY'S TAGLINE

Distill your company's greatest strengths into a catchy phrase that sells your product or service. Doing this is harder than it sounds! Think Disneyland, wrapping it all up with "The Happiest Place on Earth!" or Nike daring us to "Just Do It." What can you say that will help your target market understand how fabulous you are? The clearer you are on your other corporate branding elements, the easier this creative exercise will be!

CORPORATE IDENTITY

Without a doubt, a company's corporate identity, especially its logo, is part of its overall branding strategy. However, I'm calling it out from the other branding elements because of its uniqueness and depth of impact. Your logo is the heart of your corporate identity, not unlike a corporate signature. It projects the perfect image to your customers and prospects.

If done correctly, your target audience will love your logo. They will find it eye-catching and appealing, and will feel magnetically pulled to it with a positive emotional response. Done incorrectly, your audience will have the opposite reaction. It will unsettle your audience. They may not be able to differentiate you from your competitors, misunderstand what you do, or just not like the look of your logo so they would never consider wearing a sweatshirt or drinking from a cup adorned with it.

One of my agency's specialties is personal branding, specifically for consultants and coaches.

In Appendix D of this book, you will find a valuable array of tools to help you determine your personal brand. We enjoy the challenge of working with an individual, and it's usually less difficult to arrive at their mission, vision, and values than it is when working with larger organizations. **However, whether you're an organization or an individual promoting your personal brand, whoever is designing your logo should take into account all the above branding elements before beginning to create.**

Hundreds of books and thousands of blogs have been written about the finer points of how to create a logo. My company works with graphic designers that ask the right questions of the client, so they can arrive at the perfect logo. This includes questions like, what existing logos do you like? What appeals to you about them? What symbols do you want included in your logo? And, what are the ways you will be using the logo, which is a very important question to determine parameters. For example, some logos may be expected to appear primarily on horizontal or vertical spaces.

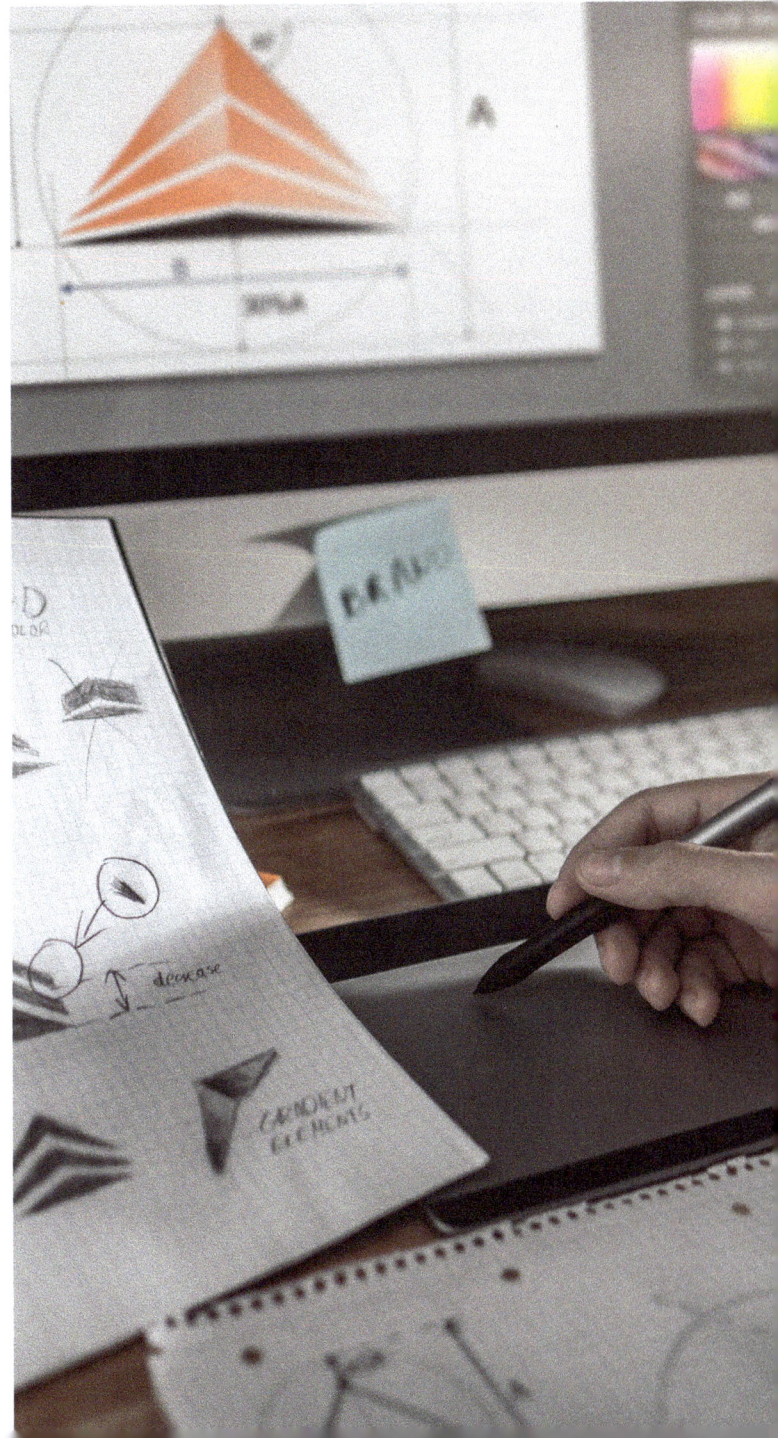

Often, we need to remind clients that the elements introduced in a logo—such as the colors, font, art, composition, shapes, etc.—should not be selected only based upon personal preference. **Decisions should be made based on the meaningfulness of each element incorporated into the design.** For example, a personal brand may easily be able to follow the favorite, most inspirational colors of the individual being branded. However, a company that wants to appear trustworthy and stable may want to rethink the use of a loopy, breezy, sans serif font for their name.

In corporate identity, as in all marketing efforts, communicating the right message is the name of the game. Your corporate identity should clearly match the image you want projected for your company. When your graphic designer brings you drafts of your new logo, don't get distracted by the one in your favorite color. **Evaluate them by which one best represents your company and communicates your brand strategy based upon your company's mission, vision, values, and USPs.**

Then, with your corporate identity solidified, you are ready to blend your logo, colors, design elements, etc. with your other foundational marketing ingredients—your website, social media, and print collateral.

WEBSITE DEVELOPMENT

We've already discussed how not everyone has a website. Of those businesses, 35 percent feel their operation is too small to warrant one. (Horne 2021) However, I think it is simply foolhardy not to have a website. Not only will a website allow you to be found on the web for your products and services, but it presents you as a serious professional.

I don't know anyone who would hire someone who did not have a website unless they had a personal relationship with them. That means if you intend to generate clientele beyond family (or one major client), you'll need to do something about your online presence. A website is a great place to start, and in my opinion, an absolutely essential foundational marketing ingredient to be competitive in today's marketplace.

With the draft of your corporate branding elements and logo in hand, your next step is to envision and consider the needs and main objective of your website. What do you want people to ultimately do after visiting your website? Is it just a glorified business card or do you want them to immediately fill out a contact form? Pick up the phone and call? Make a donation? **Every decision you make in the website development process should lead the site visitor to your ultimate "call to action."**

There are many types of websites. Styles and navigational trends come and go and a good website developer can help you produce a website that looks modern and performs well. Unless you are developing the website yourself, you should be working with someone who will ask the right questions to determine your needs.

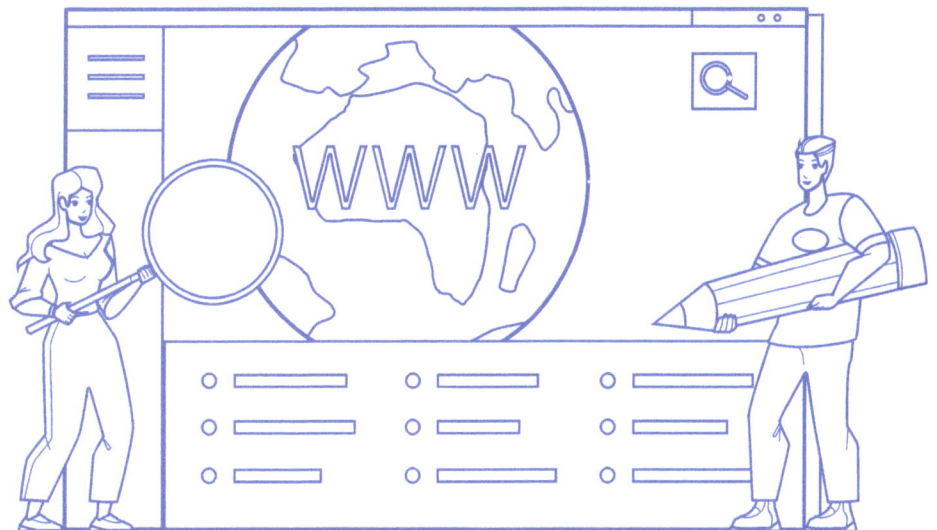

Know that there are plenty of ways to use your website and, depending on your product or service, a certain type of website may be more applicable than another. On the internet, you'll find companies that use their websites in various ways:

AS A LIVING BROCHURE

Your website can be a place to present your company and what it does. It can be updated regularly if you have a business that changes often (in staff or services). Then it will also make it easy for your site visitors to take the next step, whether that's picking up the phone, completing a form or ordering online. You also may consider having more in-depth information about your company like the company mission and values, history, a photo gallery, company biographies, and/or a blog. This approach to websites is popular with business to business (B2B), and particularly service businesses where developing a relationship is key.

AS AN E-COMMERCE SITE

Your site may be primarily a catalog where your customers can order. This kind of site is comprised primarily of photos, product descriptions, and order forms and is popular for brick-and-mortar stores, apps, and mail order products.

AS A DONATION SITE

Perhaps the main reason for your website is to collect donations to show support for a cause or an idea. You will see this with nonprofits or crowdsourcing sites.

AS A THOUGHT LEADERSHIP VESSEL

A site can function primarily as a way to display your expertise through regularly-written blogs and opinion pieces. Your site also may host registrations for courses or webinars from the thought leader. These types of sites are a gold mine of information for the target audience and most popular with coaches and consultants.

AS A CUSTOMER PORTAL.

Sometimes the main objective of the website is to offer a place for customers to monitor their activity and relationship with the organization. There is a portal, accessed through the website, where the customer logs in and manages their activity with the organization. These sites are commonly seen for health care, financial, and subscription-based services.

AS A PORTFOLIO HOST

If you are a creative professional, the main function of your website might be to hold samples of your work so people can get to know your capabilities. Portfolio sites are necessary for artists, graphic designers, web developers, content writers, musicians and other creative professionals.

As you can see, your particular website may combine any and all of these components, but you will still have one main, major call to action that needs to be considered as the site development moves forward. Make sure yours is crystal clear so you can make the right decisions for your needs.

SOCIAL MEDIA

Social media isn't just for the average joe anymore. It should be included as part of your foundational strategy. It's usage in business, not only with advertising but also in engaging companies through regular posting has been unprecedented, even for B2B companies. In fact, research has shown that **55 percent of B2B buyers search for product/vendor information on social media and 75 percent of B2B buyers** and **84 percent of executive-level personnel use social media to help make purchasing decisions.** (Horne 2021). The platform you choose (Facebook, Instagram, Twitter, LinkedIn, Twitter, Tik Tok, etc.) will clearly depend upon your target audience and your ultimate call to action. Every platform offers a specific brand advantage for every business, and different advertising capabilities, too.

For example, do you have a very visual product and a dedicated fan base? Instagram may be for you. Do you make fabulous video and seek a younger clientele? You may belong on Tik Tok. Looking to reach business CEOs with your business expertise? Start working LinkedIn. There's something for everyone!

Just like the perfect recipe, though, your foundational marketing efforts must be done in order. Begin with your corporate branding and create your website before you launch your social media strategy. You want to be able to send all those social media followers to your website, and you'll want to get all those social media icons on your home page!

PRINT COLLATERAL

Even with all the digital assets we have at our fingertips these days, there is still a place in our world for a well-designed, branded business card or an attractive brochure, catalog, or sell sheet. These also are foundational marketing efforts that help us to introduce ourselves to customers.

The kind of print collateral you need is completely dependent upon your needs. But here is a sample of those you may consider:

BUSINESS CARDS

Whether a physical one or a digital exchange of information, business cards are a quick and easy reminder after an in-person meeting and is like a passport into someone's contacts.

CORPORATE BROCHURE

Best created after the website, using similar content and images for consistent branding.

CATALOG

If you have an e-commerce business but work with sales representatives, a catalog may fall under the category of your foundational marketing efforts.

SIGNAGE AND BANNERS

If you have a brick-and-mortar operation, on-site signs and banners will help entice customers and move your goods. These foundational marketing tools will be a priority for you, from the sign on your door to your point-of-purchase advertising.

As you can see, foundational marketing is the first and most basic type of marketing that every business needs to be successful. In the next chapter we will discuss the second of the Golden Five that will give your marketing structure to build your audience. We call it **executional marketing.**

CHAPTER 5

EXECUTIONAL MARKETING

The woman who sat before me wasn't a typical entrepreneur; she was an entrepreneur by misfortune.

Since the untimely death of her brother three years prior, she had become the leader of his packaging company. Up until that fateful day, she had been working in accounting. Then, in what seemed like the blink of an eye, she was in charge. Now, not only was the fate of the company and its employees riding on her, but also the fate of the legacy that her brother had left. She wanted to honor him by keeping his business running successfully in the fiercely competitive marketplace.

The company was doing ok, but something was missing. They had a solid customer base and a good reputation. They had their foundational marketing pieces in place—a website and some collateral material. They even had some social media accounts, although the company admittedly did not post in any strategic, frequent way.

I listened patiently as she explained what she wanted for the company. More of a presence with clients. Better prospecting. And overall, a stronger sales pipeline.

I knew immediately that what my client's packaging company lacked was the implementation of an executional marketing program. It's yet another one of the Golden Five that every company should have in its marketing strategy.

WHAT IS EXECUTIONAL MARKETING?

A company's executional marketing efforts are the ways in which they provide ongoing, regular communication to their captive and prospective audiences. Every company needs some form of executional marketing, depending on their overall objectives. A well, thought-out executional marketing plan can help you do the following:

- Reconnect with past customers
- Stay in front of your past and present customers to remain top-of-mind
- Establish you as a thought leader
- Communicate news in a timely way

- Increase your brand awareness
- Educate your audience
- Allow prospects and current customers to engage with you directly

Most companies would look at the list above and say, "Hey, we need more of that." With apologies to all the vegetarians out there for this metaphor, your executional marketing is the meat of your strategy. It's one of the most important parts of your efforts because it is ongoing and eventually, expected, demanded, or even eagerly awaited by your audiences. Without it, there's just something missing from your marketing. Your prospects and customers may miss it, too. And while you may not know it, they may be getting what they hunger for, like educational blogs, and sales offers, fun social media posts and more, from one of your competitors instead of you!

Most, but not all, of these executional marketing efforts fall under the realm of digital marketing since most originate, are distributed, and monitored online. The term "digital marketing"

encompasses a lot of activities, but most of them definitely fall within the executional marketing category. They are done on an ongoing basis to continually engage with customers in a meaningful way.

As we describe some of the most popular types of executional marketing strategies, you'll notice that each one can achieve one or more of the objectives that we've included in bullet points above. **Again, a company that ignores some of these very effective executional marketing strategies may be missing opportunities and leaving money on the table.**

What are the components of a good executional marketing strategy? Let's take them one by one.

SOCIAL MEDIA

Social media was mentioned as number one of the Golden Five because set-up of accounts is your first step. Keeping it steadily supplied with content is an executional marketing strategy. And whether you love it or hate it (and we've met business owners in both camps), social media is here to stay.

Your efforts will pay off. Studies show that 97 percent of Fortune 500 companies use at least one social media platform to keep in touch with their stakeholders, and for smaller businesses, social media provides a very affordable way to promote themselves as well (Porteous 2021). In fact, with creativity and a little elbow grease, businesses can see measurable results without even having to resort to paid ads.

On the other end, one study of 150 Singapore businesses reported that as many as 95 percent of small businesses fail in leveraging their social media marketing to the advantage of their brand. (Yahoo Small Business 2014) The study cites several reasons for underperformance, like failing to target customers correctly. Other common mistakes include not having a proper social media URL, posting inconsistently, failing to duplicate traditional advertising success on social media, or advertising too much and not giving value.

The basic rule for social media content is 80/20. In other words, 80 percent of a business' posts should offer informational value for your audience and a mere 20 percent should push your products, services, and offers. However, depending on your specific situation, a different ratio may work for you. (Hall 2018)

Creating content, especially an ongoing, steady stream of it for social media, can tax even a large company. The best person for this job is an intrepid soul who is specifically assigned to it. They should engage with it themselves on a regular basis. If the person hired is external, make sure they are plugged into what is happening at the company in a manageable way or the collaboration will fail. **The perfect person also ideally has a "nose for news" and can instinctively spot post content and photography opportunities.** They also should like to research and to share content from other sources that would be of interest to followers on each social media platform. Finally, your social media person should work well with apps and technology (as each platform has its own requirements and you will probably want to use a scheduling software to accommodate regular postings). They also should have some skill in graphic design (to create eye-catching posts and be able to resize images for each specific platform), photography (to capture engaging corporate images or select good stock photo), videography (especially if your company is on Snapchat or other video-driven platforms), and writing skills (for creative work choice and spotless grammar and spelling). Given the range of skills needed, many businesses find it easier to outsource their social media marketing to an agency.

Before you add social media into the treasure chest of executional marketing efforts, make sure you have a strategy. Determine the following:

YOUR EXPECTATIONS FOR SOCIAL MEDIA

It's not enough to do social media to keep up with competitors. You must have objectives beyond that goal. What do you hope to achieve? How many followers do you want? What kind of engagement would you consider a "success?" How many likes, shares, etc. are you looking for per post? Per month? Will you use social media to target your audience and directly advertise to them or use it just to keep in touch? Have some metrics set and monitor your engagement closely for clues on what kinds of posts perform best. Keep watching and tweaking, based on your audience and what they like.

YOUR AUDIENCE'S LOCATION ON SOCIAL MEDIA

Determine the social media platforms that your audience frequents. For example, if you are targeting senior citizens, you can probably forgo the TikTok account. If you are aiming for teenagers, don't expect to find them on LinkedIn.

THE BEST PLACE FOR YOUR POSTS

Consider which platforms would work for your company. For example, if you believe your audience is on YouTube but you sell inanimate objects, you will have to be more creative about posting videos than the animal trainer down the street.

HOW OFTEN YOU SHOULD OR WANT TO POST

The internet has hundreds of blogs and articles from the experts on how often you should post and when. Scheduling software often automatically helps you determine the best time

to post. Answers will vary, depending on who you ask, but it is truly dependent upon by your company and your audience. For our B2B clients, we recommend posting a minimum of three to five times a week on most platforms. One way to determine the correct frequency to post is to watch your engagement and how quickly people respond. A very responsive audience may appreciate more content while a slower-to-reply audience may be satisfied with infrequent posts. Of course, you also can "train up" your audience to expect certain posts from you on certain days (i.e., Throwback Thursday posts). Our best advice is to use your capabilities and content control preferences as a guide. If you are a business owner who must see, tweak, and approve every post before it goes out, a daily posting schedule may be too rigorous for you or frustrating for the person assigned to manage the campaign.

HOW YOU WILL SCHEDULE THE POSTS

There are many different kinds of scheduling software available, but regardless of whether your effort is managed by a platform or done completely manually, you cannot be successful without having a strategy and schedule/editorial calendar for your posts. This can be done in something as simple as a table in a Google doc. For each post to be scheduled, indicate the date to be posted (time, also, if desired), content (words), image (if necessary), hashtags, and other notes about how the post should be treated.

WHAT YOU WILL POST

This is where a lot of companies get really stuck. Keeping up the social media schedule requires an underestimated amount of dedication and creativity. You won't have to look too far to find a blog that gives you "100 ideas for posting on social media," and we highly suggest you research your industry, including your competitor's social media accounts for ideas. However, for now, let's get you started with a few basic categories of social media postings.

- **Company news** like new employees, equipment, products, services, etc.
- **Industry updates and trends,** sharing news from authoritative sites that would be of interest to your followers
- **Celebration posts** for milestones, such as company anniversaries, the one millionth customer, national days, etc.
- **Sharing of company assets,** like blogs, internal resource pages, etc.
- **Ideas for use** of your product or service.
- **Series of postables** concerning your product/service. For example, a series of graphically-driven posts on why Brand Z is the best on the market. Use a fabulous, branded image of Brand Z for each post and give a new reason and explanation of each reason Brand Z is best on each post. Do one of those a week for a series of weeks, perhaps once on each day of the week.
- **Behind the scenes** at your location or with your employees. Let customers have a glimpse into your day.
- **Relevant posts from other organization's social media sites.** Don't forget to keep an eye on a finite number of sites that also would interest your followers and share those posts with your audiences. Before you share, make sure the information you are sharing comes from a reputable site. Also, make sure it comes from a neutral, non-competing site, like a collaborative partner or national association.

Remember that the most engaging posts include images, and especially video. Typically, the more eye-appealing you can make a post, the more successful it will be.

dea!

CONTENT STRATEGY

Much of your executional marketing efforts have to do with the content your company is creating and distributing. It ties into your overall content strategy. **Through the creation of original content, you can engage and communicate on an ongoing basis with your customers,** which is the whole idea behind executional marketing.

Content marketing is popular but not always executed well. According to a report by Small Business Trends, about 91 percent of B2B use content marketing, but only 43 percent have a documented content marketing strategy. For business to consumer (B2C) businesses, the numbers fall from 71 percent feeling they need a content marketing strategy to 33 percent saying that have a documented plan. (Rathore 2021)

Businesses value and respect the idea of content creation because it works. When people want to learn about a company, about 80 percent find the information they want through custom content distributed by the company, which is why three out of four B2C content marketers believe their content marketing efforts are successful. (Rathore 2021)

So, what is content marketing, anyway? It's any custom, original content that your company may produce to communicate, educate, persuade and reach your target market on a regular basis. For social media, your customers will "follow" or "like" your pages. For your digital marketing efforts, they will "opt-in" so that you can send information directly to their inbox. You're probably familiar with receiving content marketing from companies, even if you are not yet doing any for your business. They include items like:

EBLASTS

These short, to-the-point quick messages promote a sale or offer and/or make your brand visible on a regular basis. To send eblasts you will need to build a mailing list and use an email service like Constant Contact or MailChimp to design your message and have it delivered within industry regulations.

As consumer audiences become more sophisticated, they gravitate to brands that display authenticity and transparency.

The important thing with eblasts is to hit your audience's sweet spot in terms of frequency. If you send too often, they may find your communication irritating and unsubscribe. If you don't send frequently enough, your message may not have the impact you want.

Remember that anytime you are sending to a digital audience you have the capability for audience segmentation. For example, if you're a product manufacturer and need to regularly communicate with both sales representatives and the end user, you may create a different strategy for each audience. You may send quarterly newsletters to the sales reps about how the company is doing and something monthly to end users about products and services. **Customize not only your messages to each audience, but the frequency, too.**

As you launch your own eblasts, consider your own experience with commercial eblasts. What makes you want to subscribe? Unsubscribe? What companies do eblasts well? Before you launch, determine a strategy for your eblast efforts,

including your defined audience, objectives, and metrics for success. Most eblasts have a clear call to action and want the recipient to do something specific, like call for a quote, read the blog, or register for an event, which can be the clear metric for success in most cases.

Most importantly, never underestimate the power of your subject line. It must intrigue enough to get the recipient to open the email. You may even want to test a few different subject lines on a sample of your audience before sending the eblast to your entire list. That way you will be using the higher-performing subject line.

NEWSLETTERS

Newsletters are often executed identically to eblasts but contain more comprehensive information in them. They may have specific articles or sections that the customer expects and looks forward to reading. And just like your eblast planning, make sure you know why you are doing the newsletter, who it is going to, and what you will need to achieve from it for it to be

a successful venture. Again, consider audience segmentation. Who would benefit most from the newsletter? Should two versions be developed and a second version sent to a different group? Only you know what would work best for your particular industry and brand. In terms of content, your newsletter should contain a little bit of both parts of that compound word—news and a letter. That means besides giving news, take time to speak personally to your mailing list. **As consumer audiences become more sophisticated, they gravitate to brands that display authenticity and transparency.** Most consumers (86 percent) say that authenticity is a key factor when deciding which brand they like and support. (Mohsin 2020) By sharing a little bit of your (or your comany's) collective thoughts on the shared experience between your company and its patrons, you bring them into your world and show authenticity. In other words, don't forgo emotions. Express gratitude, declare hope, and even admit struggle to your audience when appropriate. Communicating to them like an old friend can cultivate a relationship that will last!

Finally, make sure that you have a call to action to your newsletter, which is typically responding to an offer or visiting the website. Which, by the way, should absolutely have a mechanism to add people to the mailing list on your website. It can be a button off to the side of your home page or on the contact page. If they're interested enough to come to your website, you want to make sure they have the option to subscribe to the newsletter!

BLOGS

If you don't have a blog on your website, you are not only missing an important opportunity to educate your audience, but also the opportunity to rank higher on Google. That's because the Google algorithm rewards websites that offer fresh content on a regular basis. **Hence, a blog can be a very valuable addition to your content marketing strategy.**

Blogs have grown longer over the years. In 2014 the average blog was 808 words and in 2020 it clocked in at 1,269 words. (Yahoo Small Business 2014) As long as the blog makes the point you want and supports it with anecdotal information, statistics, facts or a combination of all three, it is long enough for publication. **However, you really shouldn't publish a "blog" shorter than 400 words or it may not be indexed by Google.**

Your blog is not a bulletin board for your ads; it must provide valuable content because it will reside on your website. People do not search the web for ads, but for information on what your products can do for them! At its best, your blog will offer tantalizing information that can't be found elsewhere. It will answer the most pressing questions of your prospective customers and be found because people are seeking the answers.

So, can you use your blog as an advertisement in any way? Yes, but you must do it in the context of giving objective information. Let's say you are a restaurant, and you just started serving breakfast. Your next blog should not be a picture of the meal, the price, and an encouragement to come and get it. That's appropriate for an eblast, an ad, or a front-page banner on your website, but for a blog you need to do more. You could do a blog on America's most popular breakfast foods and mention in the blog that to serve these needs, your restaurant recently launched a new breakfast meal.

There are plenty of ways to organize your blog, but you will often see them in the following formats:

- Listicles (ex. Five Reasons to . . ., Top Ten Ways to . . ., Three Mistakes to Avoid When. . .)
- Checklists
- Reviews
- Case studies
- Stories of customer experience
- Curated content (opinions from different professionals)
- Survey and/or research results
- Comparisons of products/services
- Company's response to current trends

There's no end to the creativity that you can employ when you launch your blog. Just make sure that you do it with a solid strategy and always remember a call to action at the end. Remember, if your blog is found off your website by a person who is unfamiliar with your company, **putting a call to action at the bottom of the blog can drive them to your website.**

SEO

SEO/SEM AND DIGITAL MARKETING

SEO and SEM are acronyms for search engine optimization and search engine marketing. Both were mentioned previously as a potential marketing vehicle to be used, and both activities are concerned with your website's rankings on the internet. Here's how it works:

SEO/SEM agencies use a variety of digital marketing techniques to increase your website traffic. By doing so, the search engines will see your website as popular and raise you in their rankings. Then when a prospect searches for products and services like yours and they receive a search engine result page (SERP), their eyes will see your company listed higher than your competitor's and be more likely to call you first.

Working on increasing your performance in the search engines is a dedicated strategy that involves a consistent investment to see results— but the results are real and measurable in terms of increasing website traffic. In fact, **60 percent of marketers believe SEO is vital to online success**

and **82 percent observe positive effects from SEO.** (Zuckerman 2020)

About 80 percent of website traffic comes from Google. The Holy Grail of website searches is to be rated number one in the Google search engines, or at least on the first page. That's because 92 percent of all search engine traffic goes to the results found on the first SERP of their Google search. (Zuckerman 2020) Right now, the number one spot is almost always held by someone who has paid for it. You can witness this when you Google something and look at the very first result listed. It will typically have an "ad" icon next to it. But if you look further down the list of results, you will see the "organic" search results. Those results are unpaid and purely rated on their popularity and the quality of the content they offer.

Aside from the paid advertisers, theoretically, any company can rank number one in the organic Google SERPs, and sophisticated audiences know this. They respect the organic results because they have earned their top spot—not by writing a check to Google but because people have frequented their site, which means it must be worthwhile.

It's difficult for any business to aim to be number one in Google and make it there without a very aggressive and expensive campaign, typically assisted by a digital marketing company. To make progress in the search engines, agencies will suggest a plan of action with a combination of techniques, such as:

RESEARCHING AND IDENTIFYING KEYWORD AND KEYWORD PHRASES

It is necessary to work these keywords into your online content to be found more often and raise your ranking in Google.

HELPING YOU WITH YOUR "OFF-PAGE" SEO

With this tactic, you identify other places on the web where prospects can find you, like online directories and listing services. These "backlinks" will lead people to your site and increase your web traffic and popularity.

LAUNCHING AN ONLINE ADVERTISING PROGRAM

This is an incredibly effective technique, which will increase traffic to your website to improve your SEO and also convert clients at the same time. These may include a paid search (where you pay to be listed at the top of the SERPS) or pay-per-click ads, which charge you when prospects click your ad and travel to your site.

It's difficult for any business to aim to be number one in Google and make it there without a very aggressive and expensive campaign.

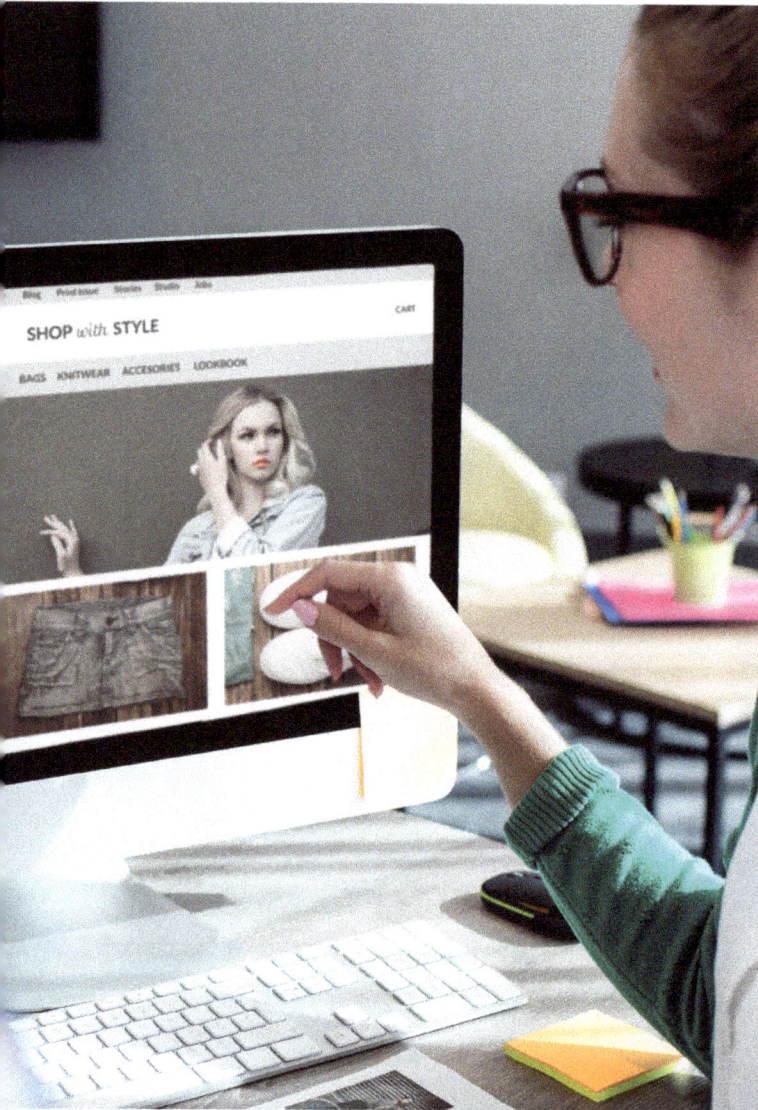

MONITORING YOUR RANKINGS

How do you know how you are ranking in Google and if your efforts are making a difference? You must monitor your progress, using Google Analytics or other type of monitoring software. With this data, you can determine which pages are performing, which are converting, and which are the weak links. As you see the activity rise and fall with your efforts, you can make better decisions about your digital marketing efforts as well as changing your website content.

As with many executional marketing strategies, you are most likely limited only by your budget and manpower to implement an excellent digital marketing program!

WEBSITE CONTENT AND BANNERS

Part of your content marketing strategy should be a continual audit of your website content. Is it fresh? Persuasive? Complete? Up-

to-date? In our experience, we have rarely worked with a client who had an established website and did not need to improve their content either in quantity or quality. Many companies "set it and forget it" with their website, but that can be a mistake. **Your organization's growth and changes should be reflected on your website.** Just imagine if your prospective client took a look at your website along your competitor's. What would they think? Who do you think they would call first?

Website banners are another often overlooked executional marketing effort. Some companies will launch a successful eblast about a new product, for example, but forget to publicize the new product with a simple home page banner. For a prospect who is not yet on the mailing list and visits your site, that banner may be the only way they learn about your new product.

Your website is a foundational marketing staple. Remember, though, that if monitored correctly and updated regularly, it also can be a powerful executional marketing tool.

LEAD MAGNETS

Question: how do you get cold prospects to get on your mailing list?

Answer: Give them something they want.

And what do your prospective customers want badly enough that they would give you their precious email address in return? That's for you to determine, based on what you know about your industry and your audience.

Businesses everywhere build their mailing list by offering pieces of valuable, irresistible content.

The purpose of a lead magnet, in a nutshell, is to build your mailing list. And the road to building a lead magnet is basically a four-step process.

1. **PLANNING.** Think about your prospective customers. What are they yearning to know? What do they THINK they know that they don't? What can you tell them about your industry that will surprise them? Excite them? Challenge them? The more provocative the information you provide, the more buy-in you will get from your

offer. Next, determine the piece of content that you will use as a lead magnet. Will your prospect find it worth providing their email to receive it? If so, the next step is creating the lead magnet.

2. CONTENT CREATION. Writing the content piece is typically done by a writer on your staff, a freelancer, or agency content writer with the research and writing skills to bring your vision to life. You also will need a graphic designer who can take the finished content and turn it into something colorful and appealing to read, using inviting infographics, compelling images, and a professional, yet accessible layout. There is no "one way" to create a lead magnet but here are some of the most popular formats:

- **eBook.** A substantial offering, well worth the price of an email address.
- **Downloadable reports.** It must promise (and deliver) access to meaty, attractive information.
- **Whitepapers.** More technical in nature, longer, and research-based than a downloadable report. Popular for science and technology audiences.
- **Infographics.** People appreciate a visually driven, colorful summary of information on a poster or document that they can easily reference to help them do their job better.
- **Quiz and results.** People love to find out how they rank against others. Don't forget to follow up your quiz participants with results.
- **Checklists.** They make life easier. Enough said.
- **Webinars.** While many are often offered free, they can still make great lead magnet offerings.
- **Templates.** Everyone appreciates a way to save time.

3. LAUNCH THE LANDING PAGE. Every lead magnet lives on a digital landing page. It advertises the offer and encourages the recipient to input their email for access to offered content.

The landing page should include specifics about the offer and three to five bullet points explaining why the content is worth it. Promote the link to the landing page by using the other executional marketing programs you already have set up:

- Use a **home page banner** on your website
- Put a link in your **newsletter**
- Send out an **eblast** with the link
- Share the link on your **social media**
- Provide the link at the end of **presentations** and **podcasts**
- Share the link and content piece with **employees** too, so they, in turn, can promote it to customers

4. COLLECT THE EMAILS AND GROW YOUR LIST. Most email programs like Constant Contact or MailChimp have plug-in pieces of software that will help you automate the population of your email list directly from the landing page. The prospect will then become part of your mailing list and continue to stay engaged with your company.

Lead magnets are a very doable, popular way to grow your mailing list and market your business, especially for audiences that need information to make smart buying decisions. If that's you, add lead magnets to your Executional Marketing toolbox.

PODCASTS

Podcasts are one of the newer executional marketing strategies used by companies and are continuing to increase in popularity. By the end of 2025, there is expected to be more than 144 million monthly podcast listeners, and by 2023, podcast digital audio usage is expected to rise 40.2 percent (Insider Intelligence 2021).

Podcasts are a great way for thought leaders, consultants, and coaches to distribute content in a regular, ongoing way. It is also a great way to reach younger audiences since 60 percent of U.S. adults aged eighteen to thirty-four report listening to podcasts monthly. (Insider Intelligence 2021)

The right podcast idea can keep you connected with your audience and become a lucrative advertising stream. U.S. podcast ad spending has nearly doubled between 2019 and 2021. (Insider Intelligence 2021) However, before starting a podcast, be sure that you have a good plan for execution in terms of frequency and content, logistics, editing, guests, promotion, etc.

Once again, have your metrics in place, too. How will you know when the podcast is a success?

YOUR EXECUTIONAL MARKETING STRATEGY

As you can tell, determining your executional marketing strategy is no easy feat. The trick is to know which types of programs would work best for your audiences, based on your industry, your product/service and of course, your available budget and workforce. The right marketing agency can be a terrific help to create your plan and get the marketing mix right.

Remember the entrepreneur who took over her brother's packaging company? She needed our help with executional marketing efforts. We began posting regularly on her social media, including her target platform, LinkedIn, where we increased her engagement 8,000 percent! We also do regular monthly blogs for her and a monthly email blast to her audiences. Recently, a customer contacted her with a bigger job than she was able to accommodate.

When you are turning away business, you know your executional marketing is in good shape!

When you are turning away business, you know your executional marketing is in good shape!

CHAPTER 6

TIME-BOUND MARKETING

My bank client didn't want to be "just another bank." The bank wanted to be known as a force in the community and an organization dedicated to diversity and inclusion. It wanted to differentiate itself from the larger banks by connecting with people in a personal way—especially with the Hispanic community of growing entrepreneurs who could use their financial products.

The bank was already communicating this message in some of their executional marketing efforts, but they needed to do something more. Something that would really call attention to their mission. Something that elevated members of the Hispanic community, and also their interest in it.

Our firm brought them the idea to create the Acts of Kindness Awards. These events were planned as a series of six award ceremonies, scheduled to be held at six of their bank locations over a three-month period, from August through October. The Act of Kindness Award was given to a person who was making a difference to the Hispanic community through their generosity and compassion. Nominations for the award were solicited from the bank's clientele, within a 30-day period. Each event was held virtually, so more people could easily attend. Plus, in addition to honoring the winner of the award, the evening also included a presentation from an inspirational speaker.

Our bank client loved the idea, and the campaign was a hit. The Act of Kindness Awards checked all the boxes: it elevated those in the Hispanic community; it honored someone who had truly made a difference in the community; and it showed the bank's interest in one of their key audiences. The next year, they expanded the idea and celebrated the bank's thirtieth anniversary by honoring thirty Latinx leaders in the community at their inaugural Latinx Community Awards. Compassionate leaders honored that night included a school speech therapist, who started a parenting resource initiative in her underserved schools, and the president of a local Mexican cultural center.

The bank's very successful initiative was well

planned and executed. **But it also worked because it brought the kind of marketing they needed into their overall strategy.** The kind known as time-bound marketing.

WHAT IS TIME-BOUND MARKETING?

Time-bound marketing is a marketing effort that must be initiated and consumed within a particular window of time. **The purpose of making a marketing effort "time bound" is to create a change within a very short period.** In almost every case, there is a "call to action" that must be fulfilled by a certain date—something that you want your audience to do. As a marketer, you are looking for your audience to respond to this call to action within a certain timeframe for the benefit of your marketing effort, which can be anything from a discount offer to a contest entry, or registration for a ticketed event.

You can recognize a time-bound marketing effort by its telltale deadline. Time-bound marketing creates a compelling urgency that reaches out to the consumer and draws them in. Most sales promotions fall into this category by expressing the true fact (or the illusion) that there is only a short-time to respond to the marketing offer. It also calls attention to the offer at the time it is most needed, like a back-to-school sale on pencils, pens, and notebooks in late August when it's time to shop for your children's return to academia. If someone wants to get in on the action, they need to respond by the deadline.

Time-bound marketing is in your corner when you want to create an aura of excitement and can be quite powerful because it is rooted in psychology. Studies show that we are driven to complete urgent tasks more quickly than mere important ones because we crave the immediate pay-off and sense of accomplishment. (Meng Zhu 2018) This is important to know as you think about how you can motivate your audience to quickly respond to your call to action.

HOW TIME-BOUND MARKETING WORKS

In the example of our banking client above, you can tell that we had several calls to action on the journey to having six successful events. There was a deadline on the submissions for the award nominations because we needed to select the winners in advance of the ceremony date. There was also a particular time when the ceremonies would take place (in fact six ceremonies at six different locations). There were deadlines for registering for each event and, of course, showing up for the event on time, too. The time-bound nature of the campaign permeated the planning. Since the awards program had a set time to take place, we allowed about six months to collect the nominations, to decide on the honorees, and to plan the virtual events.

Marketers everywhere use their calls to action to spur their time-bound marketing events into action! They ask everyone on their mailing lists, their friends, their families, their customers, prospects, and indeed, as many people as they possibly can find to do things like . . .

- Make a donation
- Join an organization
- Download something
- Nominate someone for an award
- Enroll in a class
- Sponsor something
- Write someone
- Vote
- Volunteer
- Exhibit
- Read something
- Seek help

You can apply a "time-bound" strategy to many, varied marketing efforts, depending on your objective and your needs. It's a popular, widely-used way to get people to respond.

For decades, public broadcasting stations and nonprofits have successfully been applying this concept to their fundraising drives. Although we are all free to donate to a cause at any time, fundraising drives compel us to do it within a deadline. And it works because we are all conditioned to meet deadlines! This has a scientific basis too. Deadline expert Dan Ariely, a founding member of the Center for Advanced Hindsight at Duke University, says that **having a deadline is a good way we "keep score" of ourselves.** Responding to someone's offer within the allotted time period makes us feel good. (Korkki 2013)

Such psychology fuels the secret weapon that is time-bound marketing.

EXAMPLES OF TIME-BOUND MARKETING

Our firm has hundreds of examples of time-bound marketing efforts because, in addition to marketing communication, we specialize in public relations, including the planning of special events, outreach initiatives, fundraisers for nonprofits, and special projects. **The proverbial ticking clock is always in the background of a time-bound marketing effort.** Something must be done at a certain time before something else occurs. If the marketing activities are not completed efficiently, the event host could miss out on valuable publicity and the opportunity for the marketing initiative to really soar!

Time-bound marketing and executional marketing go somewhat hand-in-hand. Why? Because once you understand your goals and needs for your time-bound marketing, you need to use the executional marketing strategies to promote your call to action to your audience. Like I said in the last chapter, your executional marketing strategy provides the structure of your marketing. It will help you fulfill your time-bound efforts, as well as many of the remaining types of marketing we will be discussing.

As you read about the examples of time-bound marketing efforts below, think about how you can use time-bound marketing for your organization or clients. Then think about which executional marketing strategies you have in place and how you could use them to encourage your audiences to respond to your call to action.

Time-bound marketing and executional marketing go somewhat hand-in-hand.

SPECIAL EVENTS

Every special event has a deadline to register, join, donate, etc. These can be successfully promoted through your social media, newsletters, or even direct mail postcards and/or on-site signups, etc. You probably already have a sense of how to best promote your event based on your clientele and prospects. Do they haunt social media religiously? Do they frequent your site, where signage or a flyer will be most effective? **The type of promotion and marketing strategy that works best for your special event is best determined by your audiences and their behavior.**

Special events can be held online or in person, sponsored or unsponsored, daily, weekly, monthly, or annually. The format is always up to you, as is the content. However, here are some of the most famous ways we have created time-bound marketing to hold special events for our clients:

- Grand openings
- Book launches
- Master classes/webinars
- Facebook live special announcements (e.g., contest winners, new management, products, etc.)
- Ribbon cuttings
- Open houses
- Award ceremonies
- Product and program launches
- Client appreciation events

Would any of these benefit your business model? Then time-bound marketing would benefit you as well.

CONTESTS

Contests all have a built-in deadline, right? Whether customers are placing their business card in a fish bowl for a free lunch drawing every Friday or sending in their ideas for the new mascot's name for a sports team, everyone knows when the winner will be announced. We have held many social media contests on behalf of our clients. For example, we helped a tile-and-granite customer to hold a giveaway during the COVID-19 lockdown. They offered a free granite countertop to someone who was going over and above to help people during the pandemic. They took nominations by social media post and made the announcement of the lucky winner on a Facebook Live broadcast. There was a clear call to action (to make the submissions by a certain date) which was time-bound so the announcement of the winner could be made online. The event was well-received and a great media opportunity for our client as well!

CROWDSOURCING CAMPAIGNS

Crowdsourcing campaigns typically have a start and end to their fundraising period. They can be successful when a client needs to raise money for a project and needs a professional outlet to do it. It is especially effective when the individual heading the campaign has an organization and wide network behind them.

One of our most successful efforts with a crowdsourcing campaign occurred when an author approached our company to help him publish his memoir. He was very well-connected within his industry of professional drag racing. We launched a thirty-day-long Kickstarter campaign to reach the $10,000 goal and managed to exceed it! **To generate donations, we used all the executional marketing strategies at our disposal to share the link and encourage his network.** We are certain that it was a triumphant success because of the time-bound nature and urgency of the campaign.

MEDIA RELATIONS AND CALENDAR LISTINGS

When you have a special event to promote, there is only a certain window of time to do it, so it makes sense to have as much outreach as you can. This includes reaching out to the press. But the media, by its nature, is time-bound and they have their deadlines, too, that must be considered in your overall marketing strategy.

Press releases and media alerts to online and traditional media need to be received by their respective deadlines in order to be printed or published in enough time to publicize your event well. The same goes for calendar listings and any other communication to daily/weekly print and broadcast media. Whether you are promoting your offer through a public service announcement or a paid advertisement, **nothing will happen for you if you do not heed the deadlines set by the media. Nothing is more time-bound than an editor's deadline!**

FUNDRAISERS

Fundraisers are notorious for being time-bound, for two main reasons. First, of course, is the urgency of the situation. Sometimes this is warranted (like in the case of raising money for a recent natural disaster) but often, the urgency is routine (i.e., part of an annual fundraising drive to reach a certain monetary goal). As mentioned before, responding to a call to help connects with our inner need to help each other and to be superheroes. One word of caution: when you put a deadline on donations or any other response in a fundraising situation, especially for a nonprofit, **make sure that the urgency of the request is proportional to the actual need.** You don't want to be known as the nonprofit who cries wolf.

MANAGING A TIME-BOUND MARKETING CAMPAIGN

Managing a time-bound marketing campaign takes five Ps: planning, people, precision, promotion, and production.

PLANNING

Planning a time-bound marketing campaign is similar to planning any other marketing campaign. Before you can spring into action, you must know how and why you are doing what you are doing. **Begin with your vision.** What do you want to achieve with your time-bound marketing effort? Set SMART goals—specific, measurable, achievable, relevant, and time-bound—which are the gold standard for businesses. (reference.com 2020)

Then ask, what will your organization need to achieve these goals? Put it all in your plan. And make it a written document. In our organization, we call this the "creative brief" for the client's special event. It outlines the who, what, when, where, and how of the event and helps us stay organized and on track as we move forward. It includes our clearly spelled-out objectives, the audiences we wish to reach and how we will do it.

PEOPLE

Looking at your creative brief, you will be able to easily formulate the team you need to conduct the event. Here are some of the most common activities that go into putting on a special event. Do you have the people in-house to do the work or do you need to outsource?

- Project manager to oversee the plan
- Securing venue (if necessary)
- Creation of event name and identifying logo/image
- Creation of invitation
- Registration procedure
- Desired media relations and online and off-line promotion of the event
- Securing speakers/presenters for event
- Helping with, preparing, or editing Microsoft PowerPoint presentations

- Registration/fulfillment management and monitoring of event participation
- IT/software for online events or technical assistance at in-person events
- Photography and videography at the event
- Distribution of press release, photographs, information, etc. following the event

Take it from us. Having every detail planned and assigned to someone competent will make your event run more smoothly!

PRECISION

For a production to succeed, all necessary preparations must be executed in order. If a step is skipped, disaster can ensue. For example, imagine if you found out that the automated registration confirmation was incorrectly set up and never tested, so nobody was reminded to come to your event! Or the IT person falls ill and nobody bothered to find a replacement—which you discover in the middle of your event when your IT fails. These types of snafus can be avoided with some precise attention to detail.

Create a calendar of deadlines to determine when each part of the plan must be completed. Work backwards from the actual date of the event. The calendar should clearly outline who is responsible for each activity. A project management software, like Trello or Basecamp, can be very helpful for you in this step and lead you towards a successful event.

PROMOTION

Remember those executional marketing strategies? Break them out now. How will you promote your "time-bound" marketing effort? Which one of these executional marketing strategies do you have in place to share the registration link and send reminders to your potential participants?

- Website banners and coming events
- Eblast
- Social media
- Direct mail
- Newsletter
- Personal printed invitation
- Media announcements and calendar of events
- Blogs
- Affiliate (partner) promotion and promotion to groups who may be interested in your event, like trade associations, networking groups, etc.
- Onsite signage/flyers

Don't forget to think about the **"dormant" executional marketing strategies** you have done in the past and could resurrect, like a social media or print advertising campaign. The timing may be right for a reboot.

PRODUCTION

When we talk about production we are talking about the day of your event. It's an exciting time—the culmination of all your hard work. If your team is assembled and ready to go, you're halfway there. The other half of your preparation is in the production schedule for the day.

Our organization swears by production schedules. A production schedule is a brief summary of what is going to happen with time stamps. It can be as detailed or as barebones as necessary, but its purpose is to be distributed to everyone involved in the event so they understand what is happening and when. Here's an example of a barebones production schedule for a virtual conference.

VIRTUAL CONFERENCE
@ 6:00 P.M.

5:30 p.m.
Speakers log in. Technology check.

6:00–6:15 p.m.
Welcome from CEO Jim Smith

6:15–6:45 p.m.
Speaker 1: Jane Doe

6:45–7:15 p.m.
Speaker 2: John Doe

7:15–7:45 p.m.
Q&A with John and Jane

7:45–7:50 p.m.
Sponsor introduction

7:50–8:00 p.m.
Closing from CEO Jim Smith

You also must have people in place to help you run the event, whether your production is online or in-person. This is especially important if you are speaking, so you can be freed up from any concerns. Consider these manpower needs and assign them if necessary.

- **A point person to address any issues that arise during the event.** This person should be someone who was integral to the creation of the event. They should be knowledgeable and able to make executive decisions quickly and independently, so the event is not disrupted.

- **For live social media events, someone to monitor and reply to incoming comments.** If you are using social media for your launch, you will want to have someone there to instantly respond to comments. We know from experience that attendees will inform you if there are technical problems with your broadcast—and they'll do it in the comments. It's important that there is someone who can acknowledge the problem for the attendees and also either fix the problem or find someone quickly who can.

- **Assistants.** Whether it's an onsite speaker who needs someone on stage to hold something for a demonstration, someone to time the speaker, or on-the-spot help with a PowerPoint, identify assistants who may be needed on the day of the event. Make sure they know their role and what is expected of them.

- **Social media correspondent.** This individual should be an expert content creator. Their job is to use your existing social media in real-time to promote the event. They can wander the event, taking photos, creating videos, performing interviews, or just tweeting out the action as it happens. They can even issue invitations to join in the event after it starts, if that is applicable.

- **Follow-up publicity person.** If you did a good job of promoting your event, you will have good attendance. And if the event was in person, you have photo ops! The promotion before the event is just half the promotion you need to do. The fact that the event took place is, indeed, news. So, use words and photos to release it to the world! Tell your readers that the event took place, illustrated by the photos and videos you took. Doing so creates the added bonus of making anyone who missed it regret it and mark the date for next year. So, at a minimum, get the story out to the following outlets:
  - Your website in the news and events section
  - Your social media
  - Your newsletter
  - Your local trade and community media
  - Your professional groups
  - Your podcast notes

Remember, your event is your own, and you are the one who knows your needs best. As you consider and implement your organization's own brand of time-bound marketing, you will discover what works best for your organization and why. Time-bound marketing is an important part of the Golden Five and one that is often overlooked, despite its immense power to connect and captivate your audience.

We believe almost any organization can benefit from a time-bound marketing effort, as well as the next two of the Golden Five. They'll put the sparkle in your marketing treasure chest.

CHAPTER 7

INNOVATIVE
MARKETING

As an agency owner, it's a delight for me when a client is willing to try something different. That was the case with one of our financial services clients.

The owners of the firm came to us after admiring the way we marketed JJR. They were seeking help in launching their new brand. Together, we delved into our brand development process. We eventually created an original new hybrid word for the name of their firm that meant kindness and gentleness, to illustrate the core values of the owners. The name also speaks to how the goal behind their business is to help clients climb to a place where they can fulfill their dreams and lead their most financially sustainable and healthy lifestyle. We created a stunning, vibrant logo for the firm, and released their new face to the world. And while our work incorporated some of the typical, executional marketing strategies needed to launch a new brand, we also offered something different. An innovative marketing strategy.

The client embraced our pitch to create a "financial journal" for their clients. The idea was to create a piece that would address the softer side of financial planning, where dreams and ideas take precedence over numbers. The content of the journal would help defuse one of our client's biggest bottlenecks—indecision among the people they served who wanted a strategy but had not prioritized their financial goals. The financial services company now presents the journal to their clients to guide them through intentional consideration of their values. The journal helps their clients journey with confidence to a place where their dreams become crystal clear and they feel empowered and excited to move forward with their financial decisions. Aesthetically, the journal is gorgeous, with a faux leather cover aching to be opened and inviting pages beckoning to be filled. And while the idea of such a financial planning journal is unique and not something typically offered by financial planners, our client wanted to stand out. And so, they did!

This is an example of an innovative marketing strategy. And executing one is perhaps the best way to differentiate yourself in any industry.

WHAT IS INNOVATIVE MARKETING?

Innovative marketing is a marketing tactic sprung from pure inspiration. It is the application of a distinctively creative idea within a particular industry. If the marketing approach is something you have not seen other businesses in a particular industry use before, you can consider it an innovative marketing technique.

Innovative marketing can be disruptive, but it is not actually the same as "disruptive marketing." Disruptive marketing is an often-heard buzz word in the industry that was first coined by Harvard professor Clayton Christensen in the 1990s. (Larson 2016) It refers to the sudden change of a practice within a certain industry that threatens the status quo in a visceral way. By contrast, an innovative marketing strategy is something unique that differentiates a business but may not actually change the way business itself is conducted. For example, the Model T Ford is not an example of disruptive marketing because there were other motor vehicles before the Model T

came along; rather, it was the idea of the assembly line and mass production of motor vehicles that was the disruption that changed the industry forever. Similarly, Uber wasn't just an innovative idea; it disrupted the marketplace because it changed the way we think about and request our personal transportation.

Innovative marketing involves looking at the challenge in a different way. It takes existing ideas and applies them creatively to the problem at hand on behalf of the client. Innovative marketing definitely involves inventiveness, curiosity, and the courage to do something different. Businesses that are brave enough to implement an innovative strategy are usually brave enough to stand out in the marketplace. They are risktakers with a vision.

> It takes existing ideas and applies them creatively to the problem at hand on behalf of the client.

HOW INNOVATIVE MARKETING WORKS

Like all good marketing initiatives, communication should be at the heart of innovative marketing. **Innovative marketing can be done for shock value, but typically shouldn't be.** The effort should be a meaningful communication of the company's deeper vision, core values, or goals. Truly meaningful innovative marketing makes consumers stop and wonder: what is the connection here? What is the company trying to communicate through this activity? For our financial services company, the journal communicated to the clients that their innermost ideas, thoughts, and dreams were important to the firm. It also communicated that writing their thoughts down would help create the best possible financial plan for them, which is always the goal of a good financial planner.

Innovative marketing works for businesses and for personal brands, too. In 2015 when I first visited a flight school to discuss their marketing needs, a passion for aviation was ignited within me. I went on to quickly earn my sport pilot license, then kept going to earn my instrument rating. (I'm currently working on others, too.) Often, clear sky days beckon me to the airport where I can take off and commune with the clouds. There's just something inexplicably irresistible about being a pilot that speaks to my soul. It's an aviator thing.

It also didn't take me long to figure out that I was quite the unicorn—a Latina in aviation. Aviation is a male-dominated industry and Latinas represent one percent of the estimated seven percent of certified private pilots in the U.S. (Tulis 2021) Over time, my love for aviation and my desire to encourage, inspire, and support other Latinas interested in aviation grew into many passion projects, including a new brand for me, a new word for a female pilot (#pilotina) and a number of innovative marketing efforts I launched to move the brand along, which I describe later in this chapter. It was easy to come up with innovative marketing ideas for my new brand. Why? Because it was so authentic to me, and so authentically me!

While innovative marketing works best for businesses when it reinforces the company's core values, innovative marketing works best for personal brands when it authentically expresses the personal attributes of the person with the brand. For example, we wouldn't expect Kim Kardashian, a fashion guru and socialite, to be creating a marketing campaign for power tools. We also wouldn't expect Dr. Anthony Fauci, director of the National Institute of Allergy and Infectious Diseases at the U.S. National Institutes of Health, to be releasing his own brand of cigarettes.

Sometimes though, when the unexpected succeeds, you can dig a little deeper and understand the innovation behind the marketing. For example, the recently released podcast "Renegades," with rocker Bruce Springsteen and former President Barack Obama raised eyebrows at first. The public couldn't understand what the two men could possibly have in common and talk about for an hour, even though they had been friends for years. Their backgrounds are completely different. Bruce grew up in a small, blue collar, white New Jersey town and found stardom in the music industry. President Obama is a Hawaiian-born, college-educated, mixed race, attorney and politician who made it to the White House. However, as President Obama explained, "Over the years, what we found is that we've got a shared sensibility—about work, about family and about America." (Quah 2021) The disparity of the two men drove listenership. People tuned in because of curiosity and they were not disappointed by what they found. Listeners heard the two men discuss everything from their family lives to the state of America and could clearly see the commonality there in the most unexpected of places. Would we call that podcast idea innovative for the personal brand of the two men? You bet.

EXAMPLES OF INNOVATIVE MARKETING

We are lucky to have many clients who received ideas for innovative marketing with excitement and an open mind. They have been rewarded for their courage in many ways, including media attention, greater customer loyalty, increased brand differentiation, and awareness. I've also personally been lucky enough to launch my own brand with many successful examples of innovative marketing.

> Coming up with an innovative marketing idea involves the proverbial "Thinking outside of the box."

Coming up with an innovative marketing idea involves the proverbial "thinking outside of the box." If you can create an entirely new and different idea, that's the best of all. But it also makes sense to adapt an already existing idea or product for your needs. For my "pilotina" brand, I've done both. I hope all of these examples inspire you with innovative ways to think about your personal or organizational brand. The sky's the limit when it comes to ideas for innovative marketing. Just make sure it's a meaningful activity that is authentic and communicates well to your target audience. Here are some ways that I did it and I highly recommend them for you, too!

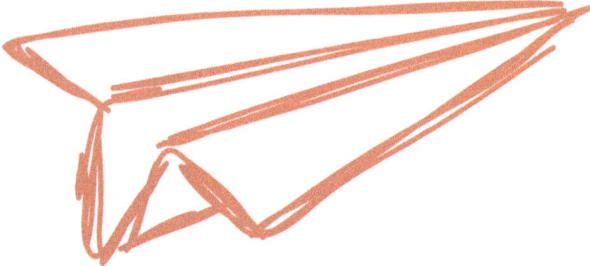

START A MOVEMENT

Behind every entrepreneur, there's a passion. By taking that passion by the horns and standing behind it, others will fall in line, too. It must not be self-serving. Your movement cannot be to patronize a store or buy a certain type of soap. But if the soap is made in an underdeveloped country and proceeds from the purchase of the soap will benefit the country's ecosystem, we may have the start of a movement.

There are books written about how to start a movement, but I have found that it all starts with seeing something that needs to change, and then stepping up to be that change. That's how it happened for me.

Years ago, I began to see a pattern in the young Latinas that I met. Often, they were not getting the mentorship they needed to reach their dreams. They wanted to attend college or pursue a career, but they were overlooked or under-coached through the college admission process. They frequently had no exposure to potential careers, outside of the people they knew. So, they became

easily discouraged and were prone to give up on a promising future, which to me, was unacceptable.

To right this wrong, I was compelled to start a nonprofit and called it *The Fig Factor Foundation*. (If you're wondering where the Fig Factor part came from, I invite you to read the memoir of my childhood called The Fig Factor, which explains how a simple fig tree in my backyard ignited my entrepreneurial journey.) The Fig Factor Foundation is designed to "unleash the amazing" in future Latina leaders. Our mission is to become a power catalyst for Latinas, ages fifteen to twenty-four, to pursue their dreams throughout our leadership training, mentorship, and powerful experiences. Together with a dedicated board of other Latina women, we wrote a two-day workshop in 2014 to activate participants with a curriculum based on eight "fig factors:" discovery, wisdom, humility, persistence, vulnerability, vision, awareness, and passion. Then we offered one-on-one mentorship to help the young ladies work towards their goals and grow by offering access to new experiences, scholarships, and local partnerships. Finally, we challenged them to give back by actively supporting a cause of their choice.

Developing this movement itself was an innovation, and a way to market an idea and gain followers. We then used more innovative marketing strategies to get the word out to the community, business partners, and politicians, too. That's the great thing about innovative marketing ideas. They beget more innovative marketing ideas!

WRITE A BOOK

Did you ever notice that politicians release a book just before they campaign? While the idea of releasing a book might not seem innovative these days, the ideas within and the format you choose can be very original. The content of your book can showcase your ingenuity or unique way of approaching a problem. The format of your book can intrigue, delight, and powerfully communicate in the simplest of ways, whether it's a modest saddle-stitched publication or an extensively designed, leather-bound volume.

As the owner of Fig Factor Media, I use

books as an innovative marketing tool, which comes more naturally to me than other marketers. Nonetheless, it is a great way to communicate and promote an idea or brand. We've successfully used this innovative marketing technique to promote JJR Marketing and Fig Factor Foundation and Fig Factor Media, throughout the years, including:

- For our corporate anniversary, we created and released small, handheld books of "notable quotes" from our client CEOs. The objective was to celebrate our CEOs and provide a giveaway of value for JJR Marketing. They were a big hit.

- We have created anthology books that bring together personal stories from individuals with a common background, set of diversities, or occupation. These began with the book series, *Today's Inspired Latina*, featuring stories of Latinas who had to overcome adversity in their lives. We went on to expand to such

books as *Latinas in Aviation, Latinas Rising in HR*, and *Latinas in Social Work* and *Latinas in Real Estate.* These books have individually elevated the authors and also their respective industries on a national scale.

- My husband and I released a coffee table book called, *Living the Amazing*, which featured beautiful photography of us together, stories from our lives, inspirational quotes, and arresting graphics. It was truly a passion project but any of our clients can get to know our values and life goals by reading the book.

- In 2021, we released the *Word Power* book series. This gift set of twelve, uniquely designed, very short coffee-table style books are written by twelve separate authors. The content of each book focuses on one single word that had significance in the author's life. The books were written to inspire others but have since inspired one of our clients in particular. They are now producing a similar series of *Word Power* books, based on their company's core values. What a great giveaway to their own clients!

- Memoirs are a great way for clients to understand the company founder and that entrepreneur's approach to business. If that isn't enough of a reason for an entrepreneur to write a book, it also leaves a legacy for their family. We've helped many private citizens and entrepreneurs transform their life and their life's work into amazing narratives.

As you can see, writing a book in any format can definitely be an innovative marketing tactic for your company. **You can make it your own in content, design, or format.** And it will be uniquely yours.

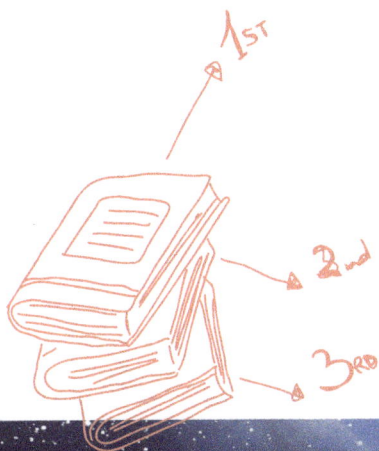

SELL MERCH

Otherwise known as merchandise, merch is an expected, favorite way of marketing for rock groups, athletic wear companies, and the entertainment industry. In their realm, it's not too innovative to have T-shirts, baseball caps, coffee mugs, keychains, etc. with the respective logo for fans to buy. In fact, it's an expected revenue stream. Can you imagine a rock concert without T-shirts? Merch promotes the brand and helps fans self-identify with their favorite role model, group, or organization. It also serves as a walking billboard. When we're talking about merch for a personal brand, though, that's where things can get really innovative.

- Remember my invention of #pilotina? I have turned the logo into beautiful pins and have used the logo on a car wrap. The pins are offered to identify the community of Latina pilots; the wrap is just for fun.

- In helping a coffee shop with their marketing, I branded a coffee blend with our company name. I have an appreciation for quality coffee!

- I took a teddy bear named Amelia in the cockpit with me on my first solo flight. Now teddy bears have become part of my *Latinas in Aviation* brand. I give them away, sell them, and co-brand them with cute T-shirts to promote other brands.

- To promote my book, *Latinas in Aviation*, I gave each of the contributing authors a beautiful neck scarf to identify them as authors at the live book launch event. The scarves matched the color of the book cover in keeping with the brand.

- Don't forget the simple standards that can be very powerful, too—stickers and badges, etc. to promote your personal brand.

In the right hands, branded merchandise can last (and celebrate the memory of your brand) forever!

CREATE AN EVENT

When we talk about special events, we are addressing a different animal than the ribbon-cuttings, book launches, and grand openings that are typical executional and time-bound strategies. Innovative marketing may be necessarily time-bound, but they also are created from scratch and, therefore, a kind of innovative marketing.

One example of this was the event we created recently for the authors and readers of the *Latinas in Aviation* community called the Latinas in Aviation Global Festival. This event took place somewhere completely unexpected—the College Park Airport in Maryland, which is the home of many aviation "firsts" and the oldest continually running airport in the world. The first festival took place in 2021 and included a fly-in, storytelling from the authors, and more fun for all ages. It called attention to Latina aviators and their contributions to aviation.

Several years ago, I launched a CEO Speaker's Series for JJR Marketing. It was an opportunity for my clients to network and learn from other entrepreneurs. For both our agency and our clients, it was an added-value and a unique opportunity they received from me, and not their other vendors.

I also created the Latina Talks and Young Latina Talks. These events were based on the famous TED Talk format, launched in 1984 and dedicated to the mission of spreading ideas through powerful, 18-minute talks. This gave some of the budding public speakers in my community a chance to practice their skills in a supportive, yet competitive environment. The best speaker among the Young Latina Talks is even awarded a scholarship, which was yet another innovative event that I created. This event was a prime example of taking an already innovative event (Ted Talks) and making it my own.

What kind of event can you plan for your clients that would celebrate their brand? Can you think of something that has not been done before? Something that will elevate others, with a special opportunity of some kind? See Appendix D for more resources on personal brands, including how to create one and how to promote it too!

CREATE AN INNOVATIVE, ONGOING COMMUNICATION EFFORT

If your cause has a strong following that you think may be ongoing, launching a podcast or magazine, online or printed, that is an ongoing communication vehicle, can be a powerful way to continue uniting your following.

The anthology of Latina pilots that we published called *Latinas in Aviation* was a big hit. So, we wanted to continue the opportunity for Latinas to tell their story. We also wanted to give airlines and industries a chance to reach the viable audience of young Latinas interested in careers within the world of aviation, as they arose.

The answer? *Latinas in Aviation Magazine.* We created the semi-annual magazine as an innovative way to promote the Latinas in Aviation brand and also provide sponsorship opportunities for companies in the aviation industry who are dedicated to building a diverse workforce. Yes, it was an initiative that took vision, manpower, and lots of hard work, but it was worth it.

GAMES

I've always been a board game player, so the idea to create board games based on some of my marketing activities just seemed like a natural step. For our large community of Latinas, were featured in the anthology series *Todays Inspired Latina* (now in its tenth volume), I developed a board game. The *Today's Inspired Latina* game pulls stories of impact from the authors using their own voices and places them within the game. Players use their imaginations to become better speakers and storytellers, just as the authors within *Today's Inspired Latina* do.

A similar attractive, interactive, innovative experience was created when we helped one of our clients create an Influencer Kit. The client was a nonprofit educational platform to help school volunteers, and the idea behind creating the kit was to forge a relationship between the founders and industry influencers. We created a beautiful box to house the custom-made, branded items for the influencers. It included a copy of the founders' book about the organization, an interactive card deck designed to create meaningful conversation, an introduction letter from the founders with a QR code to set up a meeting, a personal invitation to nominate someone for their volunteer awards program, a beautiful branded journal with pen, and the organization's manifesto to explain their mission to the influencers.

We packaged and shipped out more than eighty influencer kits to a targeted group of industry movers and shakers. The initiative made a splash and resulted in media coverage and requests for speaking engagements and podcast interviews for the clients. They were thrilled with the results, and we were thrilled that they were open to such an innovative idea.

GIVE AN AWARD

I love awards because they elevate people for doing good work. As a marketing expert, I also have seen how they can easily promote a brand in conjunction with the awards program. Awards programs are favorites of the media and promotion of the winners via social media can easily go viral.

Over the years we have encouraged many businesses to think about implementing an awards program. We have suggested "employee of the month" awards for businesses with a waning corporate culture but we also have implemented innovative programs for "COVID-19 heroes" with clients who are prominent in certain communities. We encourage nonprofits to honor their "Volunteer of the Year" or businesses that support the cause. For companies longing to make an impact in their industries or local communities, an awards program can make the splash they are looking for!

DECLARE A SPECIAL DAY (OR WEEK)

As humans, we love to celebrate and often we're just looking for an excuse to do so! Just take a look at a National Days calendar. We have a reason to celebrate every day! So, why not establish your own celebratory day related to your cause, your industry, or your business?

In the most formal sense, this can be done by seeking a city proclamation and building a

media event around the announcement. We did this as we launched The Fig Factor Foundation, our nonprofit for young Latinas. We were able to secure a declaration of April 11 as Young Latina Day in several cities in the Chicago area. The media loved it and the event went far in raising awareness of our cause and creating a wonderful buzz for our community.

On an informal basis, you can commandeer a day and christen it through your social media. On that day, give your followers a call to action and have them use their selfies and hashtags to "celebrate" the day. This kind of innovative marketing is fun and builds great community!

DEVELOP A GESTURE

I don't know how it started. One day, while I was channeling my inner "pilotina," I bent at the waist, lifted one leg off the ground and let my arms fly out wide on either side of my body for balance to look as much as possible like an aircraft. The "pilotina" bow was born. Now, I use it all the time. I encourage my fellow Latina pilots to join me in the pose for pictures. And it's a little thing, but it's a one-of-a-kind, unique gesture that definitively represents my brand.

For you and your brand, it will probably be different. Maybe it's a special signoff catch phrase on the podcast. A tip of a hat on a video. Wearing an article of clothing a certain way or a certain article of clothing every time you're in front of a camera. The size of the gesture is not the point. It's the innovation of it that will make it completely yours.

CREATE A FLAG OR BANNER

Recently I was helping a history museum honor its "100 Local Women in History." I offered an innovative addition to their marketing efforts. I suggested we create flagpole banners of the women honored and place them on the main street along the way to the museum. The banners turned out beautifully and were a great vehicle to entice people to the exhibit as well as the museum itself!

Similarly, if you've got a logo, you can create a flag. It's an innovative way to support your brand that also may make an aesthetic statement outside your headquarters or in your community where you are making an impact. If what you're doing is working, let it soar in the wind!

I've given you a few categories of innovation but undoubtedly, as you consider your clients and their needs, you will come up with your own innovative marketing ideas as well. If coming up with something innovative is daunting, consider imitation, the sincerest form of flattery. **Adapt an existing idea for your own purpose.** After all, where once calling a taxi by app was a new concept, now we get food delivery, secure city parking spaces, shop for groceries, and find dogwalkers all on location-based apps. What kind of innovative marketing idea can your business or cause take advantage of to build your audience, make an impact on your community and advance your marketing goals? Innovative marketing is the one of the Golden Five that can round out your marketing strategy in unexpected, awe-inspiring ways.

There's just one more type of marketing left in the Golden Five Framework and it's a very special one. Cause marketing.

CHAPTER 8

CAUSE MARKETING

All cause marketing initiatives begin with love, a vision, a cause, and a strategy.

One of my most successful cause marketing initiatives began on April 11, 2017. Now, every April 11 is special to me because it happens to be my birthday. But this year, it was especially remarkable because it was the same day that I was invited to attend a city council meeting for the city of Aurora, Illinois. I was there to pitch them an interesting idea. I wanted them to declare a Young Latina Day in the city.

How did I get there, you might ask? The idea for Young Latina Day came to me in what I call a "divine download," or an idea so strong, I have to move mountains to manifest it. You may remember me mentioning my launch of the nonprofit, Fig Factor Foundation, and how it "unleashes the amazing" in young Latinas, ages twelve to twenty-five based on four steps to Latina leadership: activate, receive, grow, and share. The girls in the program then work with successful Latina mentors to gain access to scholarships, opportunities, and to guide them to becoming the best version of themselves.

We already had our foundational and executional marketing in place but were looking for something more expansive to raise awareness for our cause. I felt that Young Latina Day was the answer. I felt confident that with the right support, we could make Young Latina Day not only a wonderful way to elevate the good work behind the Fig Factor Foundation, but also an excellent cause marketing opportunity for local businesses that would wholeheartedly support our cause and mission.

That day in the council chamber, I was accompanied by a few of the young Latinas from the program who were wonderful representatives of the Fig Factor Foundation. Suddenly, it was our turn. Standing tall, I introduced myself and the young ladies with me. I enumerated the modest achievements of the first cohort of young Latinas, who had recently graduated from the Fig Factor Foundation program. With passion, I reiterated the importance of encouraging the young, especially those with cultural barriers in the way

of their success. The council listened and it didn't take long to come up with unanimous approval to declare a Young Latina Day in the city. We rejoiced!

The next year, we were determined to spread the news far and wide that April 11 was Young Latina Day. We obtained agreement from three Chicago area suburbs to make the proclamation and hatched a plan to make an "inspirational tour" to the various locations on the magic day, April

11. But for that, our nonprofit needed support. We developed an inviting sponsor kit and got to work finding businesses willing to elevate their brand as part of our efforts. We were successful in getting enough corporate support to make the tour possible. Our sponsors included insurance agencies, the local chamber of commerce, consultants, service organizations, and law firms. We also had many marketing partners who helped us get the word out with their own promotional

efforts. These included our hosts along the way in Aurora, West Chicago, and Berwyn as well as Fig Factor Media, my publishing company.

In 2018, we found more sponsors to support even bigger plans. We rented an "inspiration bus" to carry our board members and Fig Factor Foundation young Latinas. With a festive banner hung outside the bus window acknowledging our sponsors and our mission, we stopped in several Chicagoland communities.

In 2019, logistics became quite challenging when we had buy-in from seven widespread communities (Bolingbrook, Aurora, West Chicago, Hanover Park, Bartlett, Chicago, and Berwyn) to sponsor a visit from our group on Young Latina Day. We decided to "divide and conquer" the stops with our board members. Then we realized that there were seven letters in the word LATINAS and we were visiting seven cities. So, we created foam letters spelling out LATINA. One letter was present at each different location, and the people in attendance at each stop signed the letter with their best wishes. We collected the letters in each place, and at the end of the day we displayed them at our closing celebration as a testament to the outpouring of love and support we received on that special day.

During the pandemic in 2020, we replaced the in-person tour with an incredible all-virtual outreach. I transformed my home into a broadcast studio and we reached out to our network of supporters who had now expanded beyond the U.S. borders. Using Facebook live, we put together a program of fifty speakers, known as "inspiration agents," as well as the foundation's board members and graduates from the United States, Mexico, Italy, France, Germany, Netherlands, Sweden, United Kingdom, Belgium, Colombia, Spain, Portugal, and Canada. The event attracted nearly 25,000 people and garnered more than 12,000 Facebook views, nearly 1,000 comments and 217 shares. That was a lot of increased awareness for the Fig Factor Foundation, but also a tremendous outreach for our sponsors!

And that's the secret of cause marketing. It elevates a brand or organization even as it elevates the cause itself.

CAUSE MARKETING DEFINED

Cause marketing is my favorite kind of marketing. There are many definitions of what it means, but here's my short and simple one. Cause marketing provides a key partnership between a for-profit and a nonprofit organization that yields growth opportunity and awareness for both.

At my agency, we encourage our clients to partner with nonprofit agencies whenever possible, and we have become known for our ability to foster these partnerships for mutual benefit. The first ever cause marketing campaign was attributed to American Express in 1983. In support of the restoration of the Statue of Liberty, they held a three-month campaign where they contributed a penny every time their card was used for a purchase. The company found the usage of their card rose nearly 30 percent during the campaign period. (Gottlieb 1986) Both Amex and the Statue of Liberty shone a little brighter for their efforts!

> Cause marketing provides a key partnership between a for-profit and a nonprofit organization that yields growth opportunity and awareness for both.

Ever since, companies have been launching cause marketing campaigns and consumers have been responding to them. In fact, studies show that 79 percent of Americans say they feel a deeper personal connection to companies with values similar to their own. And 88 percent would purchase products or services from that company. Seventy percent said they'd want to work for that company. (Porter Novelli/Cone 2019) This is why cause marketing has become a trend, with the social climate continuing to challenge brands to take a stand for what they believe in.

Consumers want to buy from brands they know, love, and trust and ideally, are aligned with their own values. This is true whether the consumer is a prospective customer or an established one. **Cause marketing helps nurture that familiarity in a visceral way.** People feel a shared, common bond with a brand that espouses their values.

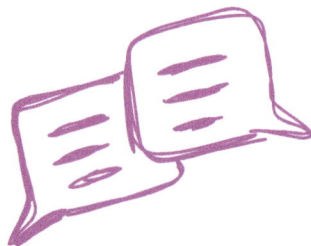

Cause marketing also provides lots of benefits for the parties involved. The nonprofit receives increased visibility for their cause and more donations from a new funding source and supporters. Meanwhile, the brand supporting the nonprofit benefits too. They soon recognize tangible as well as intangible results from their cause marketing. These include:

- Higher esteem in the eyes of the customer for their efforts to support a cause
- Market advantage in gaining prospective customers who seek socially responsible brands
- New and/or increased sales from established friends of the nonprofit
- New and/or increased sales from customers who want to begin supporting the nonprofit
- An alignment with a greater purpose, which can unify staff and assist in recruiting new talent to the company

- Synergy with the community and other efforts taking place on behalf of the cause
- Media story potential and opportunities, as they arise
- Appreciation and possible recognition from the nonprofit itself
- Forming a positive corporate identity with the nonprofit and a reputation for being a solid supporter of the cause

You are helping elevate a brand by aligning them with a nonprofit.

HOW CAUSE MARKETING WORKS

I think of cause marketing as an effort that elevates a brand as it elevates the nonprofit, even if that is simply through sponsorship. Others, like Joe Waters, a cause marketing guru who founded the Selfish Giving blog, defines cause marketing differently. He suggests that cause marketing is different than sponsorship. With cause marketing, both the brand and the nonprofit companies profit in the end, but neither receives money outright. (Karst 2020) In other words, instead of offering a sponsorship or a donation, the dollars contributed to the brand and nonprofit are provided by the consumers, through patronage or purchase. However, I see cause marketing existent in both cases. Whether you're supporting a brand through sponsorship or donating a portion of the profits from a sale, **you are helping elevate a brand by aligning them with a nonprofit.** It's all cause marketing. And the definition isn't as important as the outcome. In either case, the brand is taking an amazing step to make the world a better place!

Cause marketing is a win-win. It's a feel-good strategy that, in most cases, can't lose. However, when you're ready to jump into cause marketing, be careful with one of your biggest decisions—the cause itself. Remember that your customers are watching—and judging—your choice of organization to support. What they want to see most from your brand and nonprofit cause marketing is authenticity. Since profit is everyone's goal, they want to make sure that the cause you are supporting truly shares the values of the company or brand. If your reason for the cause marketing is only to make more money, people may resist. Most can smell "BS" a mile away. Instead, they are inspired by selflessness, passion, and the experience of being at the epicenter of something that is bigger and more impactful than they are.

Many brands have done a great job with their cause marketing efforts in this regard. Take Patagonia, the outfitter that sells us the all-weather apparel we need to explore the great outdoors. Their website proclaims that "they're in business to save our home planet," and their corporate actions show it. Their self-imposed "Earth tax" is their commitment to returning one percent of their profits to support environmental causes. They are highlighting athlete/activists who love their products and work to preserve the planet. Patagonia also resells their gear, which is a very atypical effort on behalf of a clothing retailer, yet a very environmentally conscious move. In doing so, they prove their sincerity by going above the sale of a new coat and instead helping customers recycle theirs and rewarding them with a store credit. The whole effort is better for the planet in the long run and, once again, in perfect alignment with their values. **They are living out their corporate mission.**

Another incredibly successful cause marketing effort is the (RED)™ initiative. With the support of such heavyweight brands as Apple, Starbucks, Nike, and Converse behind it, a portion of the profits from (RED) products goes to fight the world's biggest health emergencies between several global funds. The collective effort has raised more than $465 million for the Global Fund to eliminate HIV/AIDS through certain (RED) products, which are usually colored red. Some recognize that the genius of their campaign, at its core, is something small but powerful—the color red—which demands attention and action. (Motivate Design 2017)

One big brand that provides a study for us in the opposite direction of perfect alignment is the cause marketing effort of the Susan G. Komen for the Cure® with KFC. Back in 2010, the purveyor of fried chicken aligned with the cause, which raises money for breast cancer research. For every "pink bucket" of chicken sold, KFC was to donate a portion of the profits to breast cancer research. To consumers, the relationship made no sense since fried foods like the chicken KFC served up were linked to obesity and other health problems. Within two days, Komen was under fire. The effort was termed "cause dissonance" and Komen was criticized for straying from its mission, even though the organization explained its efforts as an awareness, not health care campaign.

In the end, Komen's decision to partner with KFC damaged its reputation by undermining the organization's credibility, eroding its authenticity and alienating its supporters. (gettingattention.org 2021) **The moral of the story is to make sure that the nonprofit you align with creates a synergy, rather than a dissociation, with your brand or company's products and services.**

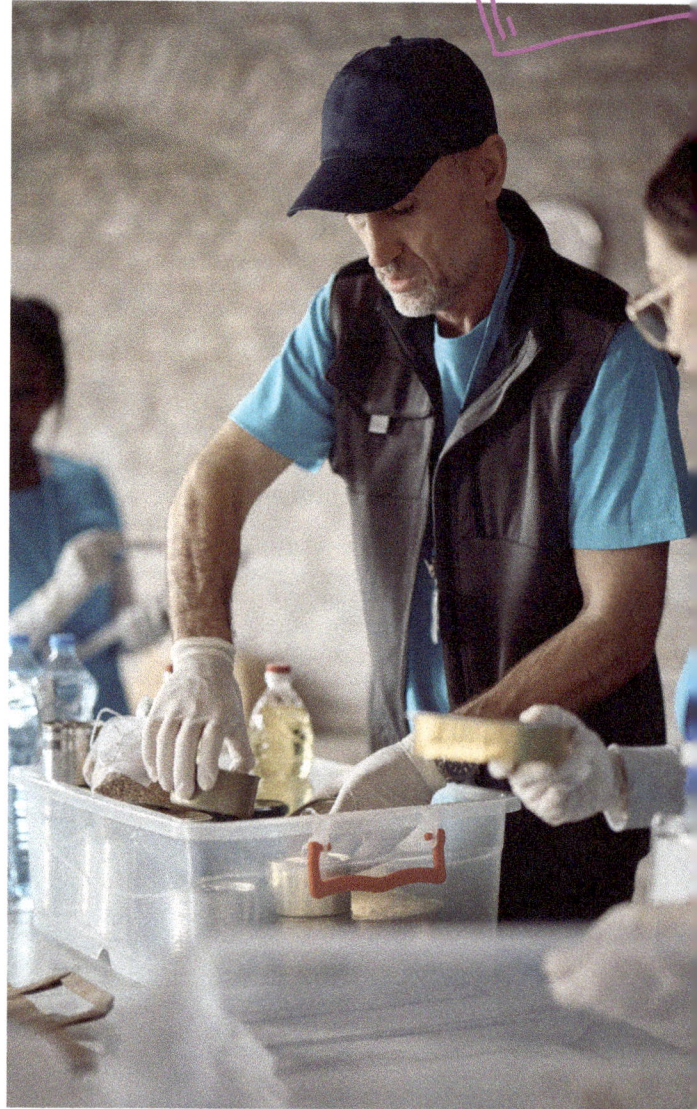

TYPES OF CAUSE MARKETING

There are as many ways to implement a cause marketing program as there are causes out there. But here are some tried-and-true favorites that you might want to consider to mutually elevate your brand and your favorite cause:

POINT OF SALE

Have you ever been checking out at a brick-and-mortar store or an online store and been asked to "round up" or give a certain dollar amount to a particular cause? Point-of-sale cause marketing is very popular and very effective because it is easy, convenient, and typically asks for a very small amount of money to make an impact. As human beings, there's nothing more irresistible than making a difference, especially when it is not a big sacrifice on our part.

TRIGGERED DONATION

A triggered donation is a donation that takes place from the brand upon some sort of customer action. For example, if the customer takes a specific action, the brand will make a donation to a specific cause. The action can be anything from purchasing a certain item to shopping at a certain time, or trying a new brand or service. **Triggered donations give the customer a feeling of self-satisfaction because their actions have made something good happen.**

As human beings, there's nothing more irresistible than making a difference.

PRODUCT LICENSING

Once again (RED)™ offers us an example, this time of product licensing. The supportive brands use the nonprofit's brand and intellectual property (like their logo) on their product. When the licensed product is purchased, a royalty is given to the nonprofit. Although this is typically a tactic for larger companies since it involves legal agreements with manufacturers, there are licensing agencies to help nonprofits market this way.

You also could create your own products. My little teddy bear, "Amelia," who flew with me on my first solo flight, has helped me raise thousands of dollars in aviation scholarships through co-branding and distribution to people all over the world. In my case, the product was very personal to me and in complete alignment with my core values, even as it helps me raise money for a cause.

MESSAGE PROMOTION

Brands and companies can use their resources to help market a nonprofit organization as an innovative alternative to a flat donation. On their packaging, signage, and in other places, brands can help communicate their support of the cause. They can use the logo of the cause or their slogan, with a declaration that the brand supports the cause. Such a campaign lets everyone know what the brand supports, which can oftentimes tip the scales in the brand's favor when a consumer is faced with a tough buying decision.

DIGITAL PROGRAMS

In 2013, Amazon launched the AmazonSmile program. It's a prime example of a digital program that provides "easy money" for nonprofits because Amazon does the asking. They encourage shoppers to choose a charity to support and to log into AmazonSmile to make it happen. Then as supporters do their regular shopping, a portion of their proceeds is automatically donated to the nonprofit's account. That's it. The cause does not have to visibly ask for donations or license any products. Money is donated to the charity when the shopper selects the charity on their AmazonSmile account. For the nonprofit, the registration process for charities is also straightforward and inclusive, which explains the popularity of such digital marketing programs.

EMPLOYEE ENGAGEMENT

Many companies and brands help their favorite nonprofit through employee engagement. **Studies have shown that cause-related marketing enhances employees' admiration for their company that in turn, promotes engagement.** (He, Chao and Zhu 2019)

One way to strengthen your cause marketing efforts is to involve your employees. What causes do they support? What causes do you think make the most sense with the core values of the company? Create a way to involve them so as a group, the employees feel heard. Take nominations or put it to a vote. Supporting a charity is a big company decision and one that employees would gladly help make.

Next, decide how to get the employees involved. There are lots of ways a company can encourage their employees to support a cause. They could offer employee time off to volunteer with the charity or hold a company-wide fundraiser, like a 5K run. Maybe employees would prefer to make a small donation from their paycheck to the cause or run their own mini-social media campaign to encourage donations. In the days when formal attire was required at the office, employees would pay to have a "casual" day. With the proliferation of home offices, we may offer a creative alternative like "no camera" Zoom days or a contest for a home-delivered meal to the employee who can secure the most donations for the cause in a single campaign. **Employees also may come up with their own creative ideas, based on your company and your corporate culture.** The point is to get employees engaged and active in your cause marketing. Working together to support a cause becomes a team activity, which benefits both the cause and the team spirit at your company.

EVENT MARKETING

Events are great opportunities to align with a cause. Whether your event is an open house or a seminar series, you can make the entire event more meaningful if it also benefits a cause in the process. You can ask attendees to bring donations to the event or promise to make a donation if they do something particular before, during, or after the meeting. Of course, if it is a ticketed event, you can give part of the ticket price to your cause.

Years ago, when we were representing a local water park, we connected them with a nonprofit that gives hope to children who have lost their parents due to homicide. The water park generously donated a day's admission to the group from the nonprofit and their generosity was rewarded with media mentions for their generosity. We also had on-site signage welcoming the group. Many people discovered the organization that day so that they could continue to support it in the future.

Another successful cause marketing effort took place between the community I built through my *Today's Inspired Latina* (TIL)series and Estee Lauder. The renown cosmetic retailer reached out to Fig Factor Media, publisher of TIL, to create an event to support the Latina community. Its "why" was to support women leaders in the Hispanic community and bolster an organization that champions the next generation of Latinas. Together, we put together a partner event called *Bellezza*, which means beauty in Spanish. The evening took place at a local Macy's department store, and included makeovers and demonstrations, as well as discounts for the attendees, who were mainly authors of the TIL series. That evening, more than 150 ladies turned out in droves and each walked away with a beautiful Estee Lauder lipstick, engraved with the hashtag ELxTIL (their initials and ours). Partial proceeds from the evening's sales were returned to the Fig Factor Foundation for the advancement of young Latinas. And that evening, a megacompany went a long way to befriend our fledgling organization, which

works to serve the community they wish to know better.

I also have discovered some innovative ways to cause market related to my publishing house, Fig Factor Media, and the authors I work with. Because I offer marketing to my authors as well as publication of their books, I often find ways to connect my authors with nonprofits and establish cause marketing efforts for them. Not only do I connect nonprofits with authors, but I also bring in a third leg of this heart-built stool, the for-profit organization. I triangulate the benefits, to create success for the for-profit company, an author, and the nonprofit. Here's how I do it.

First, I ask the for-profit company to purchase several copies of the author's book on behalf of the nonprofit. Next, we hold a special event at the nonprofit, sponsored by the for-profit organization. At the event, the author speaks and then signs and hands out her books to the attendees from the nonprofit group, making it clear that the books are available on behalf of the for-profit company. Three parties are involved and they all benefit!

The first time we tried this idea was with an accounting firm client that was looking for more community outreach. They donated copies of a book that dealt with money management to be distributed at a book event that was held at the nonprofit's headquarters. **The nonprofit was helping people with their financial literacy, so it was a perfect fit for their clients.** The author appeared for the event and gave a short address about the information in her book. We also distributed a press release on behalf of the for-profit organization, which got them well-deserved media attention. The result? A win-win-win. The for-profit company was recognized for their sponsorship of the books, the author reached a new audience who received her book, and the nonprofit offered something of value to the people they served, at basically no cost to them. Everyone was happy! We've done this on several occasions with different types of books, in various locales, with a variety of authors. **It never fails.**

CAUSE MARKETING WITH CARE

As mentioned before, missteps in a cause marketing campaign can backfire. Your relationship with any cause is not unlike your relationship with a client—you should proceed with intention and strategy. The process itself is really only three parts, but each requires a great deal of thought and synergy with the cause partner.

First, identify a proper nonprofit partner to support. Don't forget the most important thing: their interest must align with yours so your relationship will not confuse your audience. What cause has a mission that you truly want to be part of? If you are making this decision from the heart, not the wallet, you can't make a bad choice. Stay authentic, and you'll be successful.

Second, generate ideas and plan for the cause marketing effort. Here be sure to marshal your own resources and those from the charity. Undoubtedly, they have worked with partners before and can guide you towards what has been successful in the past. Be open to their suggestions but make your parameters known to them as well.

The best relationships are formed when both parties are transparent about their expectations.

As you make a plan for your cause marketing initiative, put it in writing and make sure you clearly spell out the who, what, where, when and why of the cause marketing effort. Be sure to include:

- The for-profit's objectives and expectations for cause marketing
- The key participants in the effort, from each organization
- The length of time the cause marketing initiative will take place
- Specifics of the cause marketing effort—who will be making the donations, when, and how
- Any legal agreements, if licensing will take place
- Expectations for each organization on how the cause marketing will be marketed and promoted

It also might be worthwhile to proactively recognize where operational "glitches" may occur between the charity and the for-profit. Discuss them in advance.

Third, execute and communicate the cause marketing effort. If you have planned well, execution of your strategy should be straightforward. However, communicating the strategy to your audiences is a step that is missed all too often in the process. There's no reason to let your good deeds go unseen!

Local and trade media flock to stories of corporate generosity to charities. I remember a great deal of media attention when we nominated our favorite cause to be a recipient of free pizzas during the pandemic. The national pizza chain had promised a million dollars in free pizza and the news story that ran that night did a great job of mentioning the national company as well as the nonprofit and all they did to feed the hungry. It was another win-win for cause marketing!

Cause marketing is one of the Golden Five you should be sure to incorporate into your overall marketing strategy. You're guaranteed to enjoy the feeling of helping others and the reactions you elicit from your generosity.

> In many cases, cause marketing is that extra special something that makes a brand stand out, and the world a better place.

WHAT AN INTEGRATED MARKETING STRATEGY TIMELINE SHOULD LOOK LIKE

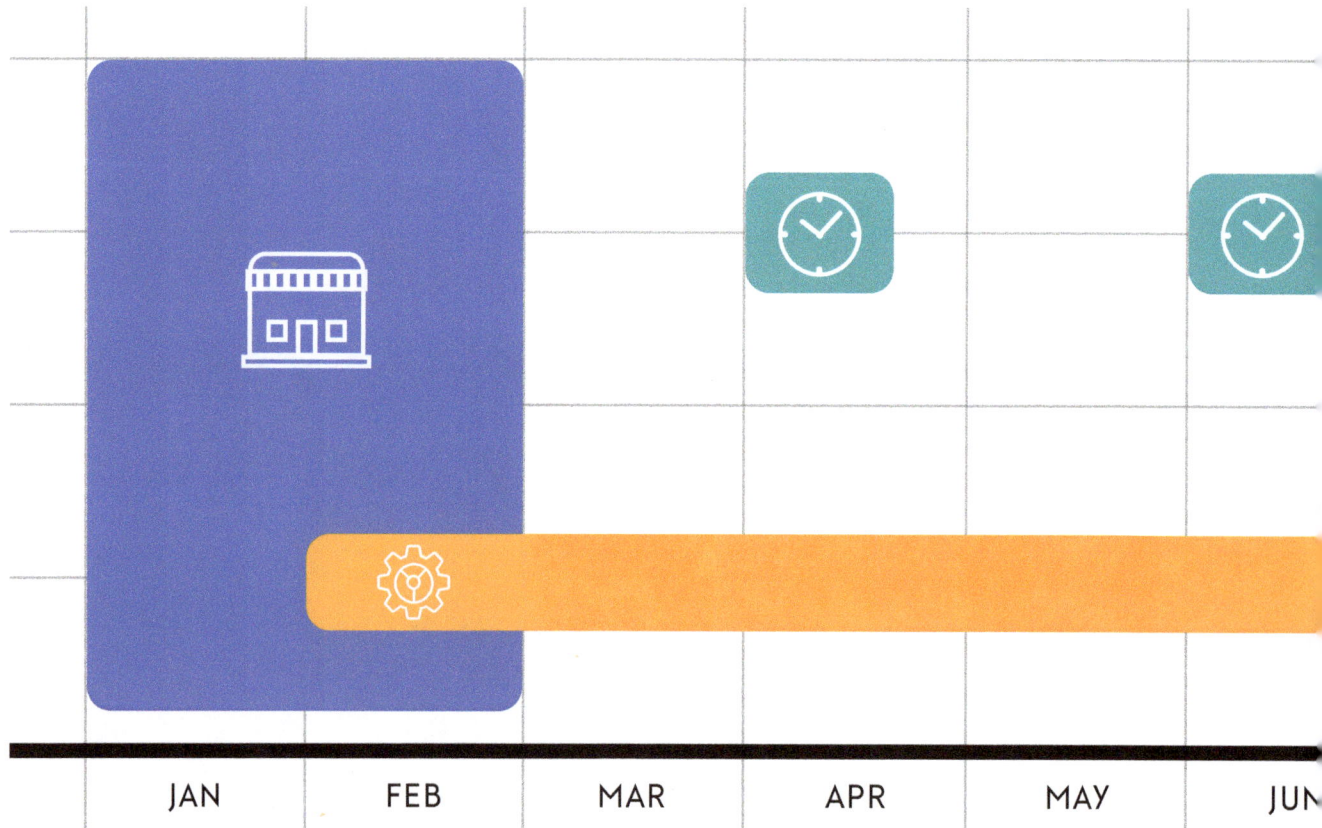

| | JAN | FEB | MAR | APR | MAY | JUN |

FOUNDATIONAL
EXECUTIONAL
TIME-BOUND
INNOVATIVE
CAUSE

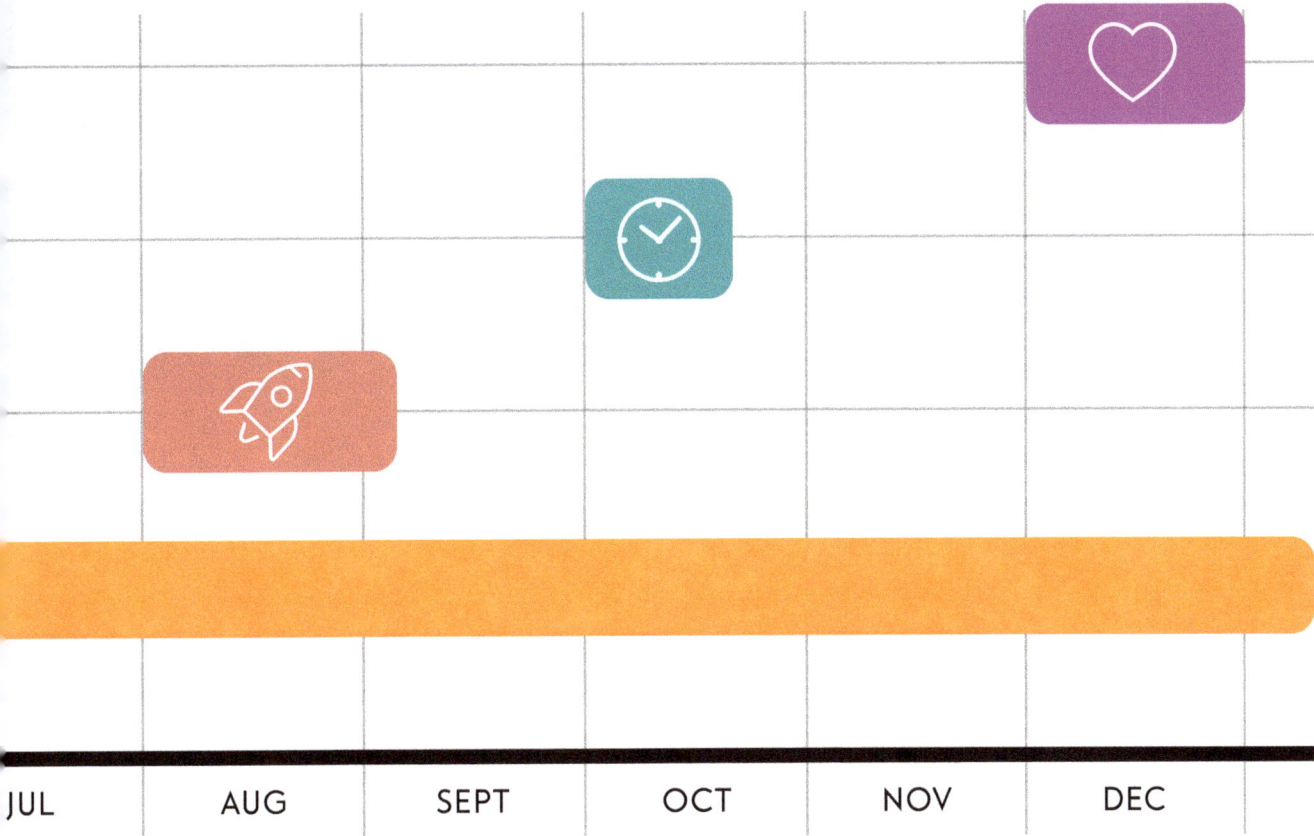

JUL   AUG   SEPT   OCT   NOV   DEC

CHAPTER 9

THE GOLDEN FIVE FRAMEWORK FOR AGENCIES

When the client called me, they knew exactly what they wanted; or so they thought. "We need help with our social media," he said. "That's all we need," he said, "social media."

I smiled politely, understanding the request, but knowing the truth that I would soon reveal to him. Social media most likely wasn't his only need, nor the answer to all his problems.

Casually, I began a discussion about his target market and his marketing goals. As always, I was searching for the pain beneath the request. I asked about his existing marketing. What else were they doing to reach their prospects beside using their underperforming social media efforts? What was their sales funnel? The call to action they were using? It turned out they were not doing much other than social media. Their expectations were very high from that one marketing channel and it was unsurprisingly disappointing them. **They were missing many of the Golden Five in their overall marketing.**

First, I took a look at their foundational pieces and found a website that appeared outdated and did not reflect the type of company they were presenting to me. This was typical for clients that were concentrating on only one kind of marketing to make it rain. It's very rare that an organization is faltering because they are missing only ONE of the five types of marketing, i.e., ONLY social media. Clients often fail to understand that for marketing to perform well, all of the Golden Five are needed, working industriously together, to reach certain, defined metrics.

This is how I came up with the notion for the Golden Five Framework. Beginning with what is often a simple request from a client, I challenge them to take a few steps back and look at their marketing efforts holistically. I try to make them see that all company marketing efforts are (and should be) harmoniously interconnected. **All five types of marketing contribute to the goals of the client, whether those types are absent or present, newly created or in need of an update.** All five must be addressed, or at least considered for best results.

THE NEED FOR THE GOLDEN FIVE

Creating a successful blueprint for marketing using the Golden Five Framework has been important for my own agency as well as the strategies I create for my clients. We have always provided services from the Golden Five but when I first started out, we tended to serve them up cafeteria-style. Now, we offer the Golden Five as an orchestrated, integrated communications plan, touching upon each of them in the precise way necessary to help our clients reach their marketing goals. By approaching marketing through the lens of the Golden Five Framework, we now help clients in a more cohesive, orderly way.

We are able to immediately spot a company that makes use of each of the Golden Five in our framework. The company has an integrated approach to marketing and follows a strategy, which maximizes the exposure of every marketing communication piece in its arsenal. The company has a process in place to automatically implement executional marketing strategies. It knows that a

simple case study content piece should reside on its website, but it also automatically shares it on social media and in its upcoming company newsletter. The company will even take that same content piece and do a case study press release for it to get it even more SEO and market reach.

Conversely, sometimes organizations are obviously missing one of the Golden Five. In those cases, the leadership sees the wound but can't find the bandage. The leadership may wonder why their competitor is doing so well in certain desirable markets and they aren't. A little research typically reveals that the competitor is engaged in another form of marketing that the other company is not. Perhaps the competitor created a cause marketing effort aligned with the target market's priorities, or an innovative campaign (like an awards program) that elevates those in the desired market. Maybe they even just have better executional marketing strategies in place, like more regular content postings than your client, or more engaging social media. As the agency and marketing expert, you can do the research and identify the deficiencies in

an organization's plan, then help your client turn the tide with the right mix of the Golden Five to regain the competitive advantage.

In the case of my client who only wanted "social media," the first order of business was to update their lackluster, underperforming website. We found that even though the social media was driving people to the website, our client was not seeing conversions. A relationship existed between the website and the social media that wasn't working. People were clicking over and clicking off, not finding what they needed, or perhaps unimpressed by the online offerings. The foundational marketing effort (the website) was not working well with the executional strategy (social media). The relationship needed fine-tuning.

I try to get clients to understand that a company's marketing efforts comprise a relationship of activities happening within an organized blueprint. Like most weak, non-existent, or broken relationships, it can't be easily fixed or strengthened with one effort. Much more is needed. It's not unlike a couple who argues over different life goals. One spouse brings home a gift as a peace offering. It's a helpful effort, which may lead to a temporary reconciliation. However, if the underlying root cause of the problem is not resolved, the issue will most likely rear its ugly head again somewhere down the road.

It's the same way with marketing. We must take a step back and look deeper into our client's pain points to find the root of their marketing challenges and then address them one by one. There is no "quick-fix" or "one-stop" solution. It takes an integrated approach, working within all their marketing channels, with a plan of action that includes the Golden Five Framework before we can begin to help in a meaningful way.

CLIENTS AND THE FIVE TYPES OF MARKETING

Agency work is ever-changing, rarely dull, and always a challenge. If you're an agency owner, I know you'll relate!

Clients come in all shapes, sizes, and levels of expertise. Some come to us with little or no knowledge of marketing; others come to us telling us what they want us to do and expect us to do what they say. At my agency, we strive to educate them all on the Golden Five Framework and the importance of integrating all five types of marketing into their efforts.

We have had clients that have never evolved beyond foundational marketing because of their lack of knowledge or resources. For these clients, we need to educate them on the power of combining one or more of the Golden Five. Doing so increases their marketing power exponentially! To use an analogy, using the five types of marketing is like the five fingers on your hand. If all five fingers are curled down into your fist, they cannot communicate. Leave the thumb up and you might be able to catch a ride into town. Put two up and you can show you're a peaceful person. Leave them all up and you have an open hand, with all fingers ready to gesture or communicate openly through sign language. Likewise, you can communicate so much better if you use more than one of the Golden Five.

We also recognize that everybody's integrated marketing solution will be different, depending on their industry, their competitive position in the marketplace, and of course, their internal resources. Although we follow the Golden Five Framework as a rule when we work with clients, the ultimate outcomes are always customized to their marketing needs. Here's how we work with clients to give them an integrated strategy using the Golden Five.

DIG DEEP WITH THE CLIENT

We begin by asking them the end result they are looking for in their marketing efforts. This takes some skilled inquiry. As with the client who "only" wants social media, there may be more to

the story than it appears. Our goal in this step is to identify what marketing efforts are in place and how they are performing. We want to ask about their competitors. Most of all, we want to accomplish the most important reason for the deep dive.

IDENTIFY THE END RESULT

If we do the inquiry right, we will uncover the most important piece of information—their end marketing goal that they want to achieve. It's that sweet spot where they want to see an increase in activity that they KNOW will result in increased sales or engagement for the organization. When we have this information, we can begin considering how the five types of marketing can serve the client.

We also do this through an online assessment. You can find a link to a page with this resource of ours in Appendix A of this book. It consists of a variety of questions that businesses can answer to determine the impact of their current marketing efforts through the lens of the Golden Five. The assessment uses the five types of marketing as the starting point of the evaluation and gives us some preliminary information on how much the company is employing these techniques. This has been very effective for clients to identify their marketing weak spots. One business that took the assessment received a score of 35 percent (clearly a failure!). It prompted them to call us and we could clearly see from the assessment results that there were specific areas of the Golden Five where we could help them grow their reach. The assessment convinced them of the need for our services, and it gave us an intelligent place to start our conversation.

INCORPORATE THE GOLDEN FIVE

Once we've come up with the goal we are working toward, we can consider the Golden Five that will help the client. Typically, when we do this, one kind of marketing jumps out at us as the direction to take first. For example, if we determine that the client's main goal is to get more people to their website, we would most likely suggest some marketing efforts that fall in the "executional" category, like content marketing or special landing pages, that drive people to action on the website. **Alternatively, if the client wants to connect with the community, we may suggest some cause marketing efforts, or perhaps an innovative outreach event.** However, even if the blueprint takes shape favoring one type of marketing over the others, we still consider the other four of the Golden Five as well. That way we can show the client the broad potential of our services, given a comprehensive, integrated plan.

1. PUT TOGETHER THE MARKETING STRATEGY

We specialize in putting together integrated marketing plans that contain a series of action items, categorized within the five types of marketing. The activities outlined will vary from client to client, depending on their marketing goals, as well as their budget and personal preferences. You can find an example of how we outlined our blueprint for one client in the back of this book in Appendix C. This is the first step in our planning with the five types of marketing on behalf of any client. It gives us an outline of the deliverables we will produce, by category. We find that our clients respond positively to this straightforward presentation of activities on their behalf. It shares our thought process and allows them to clearly see the many ways they can use their marketing resources.

2. IMPLEMENT THE STRATEGY

Next, we place each activity within a marketing calendar, so we have our implementation plan in one place. This keeps us focused on what needs to be done and by when. An example of this resource is included in the back of this book as Appendix C. However, you can use any software or project management program you wish that will keep your team moving forward with your marketing strategy on behalf of the client. By the way, it's important to share this resource with the client so there are clear expectations on both their side and yours as to when work should be completed.

WHICH TYPE OF MARKETING TO CHOOSE?

It may seem that with such a tempting smorgasbord of marketing types, it may be hard to choose the right course for your client. However, we find that between the assessment, the client interview, and a good old-fashioned research and review of competitors and efforts already in place, the blueprint often "writes itself."

Sometimes the best decision to start the client on the Golden Five Framework is to follow the path of least resistance—that is, begin with the type of marketing that is clearly missing and most palatable to the client. Depending on their situation, this can be any type of marketing. However, one of the most exciting for clients is our foundational marketing efforts.

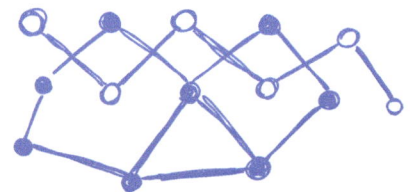

FOUNDATIONAL MARKETING: AN EXCITING BEGINNING

We have found that clients love foundational marketing efforts. Everyone is dazzled by something new and the thought of a shiny new website or slick, professional logo is always sure to impress. We love working on foundational elements, not only because they are so happily received but because it helps our clients encapsulate their brand into beautiful words, images, and marketing communication tools. As a team that thrives on creativity, it also feeds our souls. Many clients get quite emotional as they see their life's dream transformed into a tangible presentation to the world! We've even seen tears of joy. Nothing could be more satisfying than being responsible for them!

It's even more exciting when the client fully embraces the celebration of a brand refresh or a launch of a new venture in an existing company. We've had clients who have had employee celebrations with grand unveiling of the new logo itself, and clients who have launched their new brand by distributing merchandise with the new logo to the employees. It's exhilarating for the entire team and can be a real morale boost for the company as well.

EXECUTIONAL MARKETING: CREATING STEADY PROGRESS

For most clients, the introduction or launch of an executional marketing strategy creates excitement that wears off rather quickly. They love to see a new blog on their website or their cool company photos finally displayed to the world gloriously on Instagram. However, keeping up with it can be an issue, and frankly, is one of the ways an agency can be of service the most. We have the advantage of an outside viewpoint and an evergreen fresh perspective to continue offering different ideas on behalf of our clients. We also have the resources to keep our clients' social media and executional marketing efforts delightfully current, so our clients can concentrate on their core business, as they should.

TIME-BOUND MARKETING: MAKING A SPLASH

Because we are known for our special event planning, many clients come to us specifically to plan a time-bound event, like a book launch or grand opening. Even the clients that do not plan a time-bound event during the course of their engagement with us enjoy the ability to request the service, if need be.

Most companies find the hustle and bustle of preparing and implementing a time-bound event to be exciting. Events make a fabulous impact and can be easily promoted, which boosts the morale of everyone in the company and helps them see their impact in the world. Many new time-bound events also can be repeated annually to differentiate clients from their competition.

On the flip side, many clients will have objections to time-bound events. What if nobody comes? What if it doesn't pay off? ROI is always top-of-mind for clients, and time-bound events are undeniably an investment in time and resources.

In that respect, there is always risk involved. **If you detect your client is challenged by their budget or an aversion to risk, best to go easy on the recommendation of time-bound events, or help them gently work towards it as a goal for the future.** Help them visualize the best-case scenario. Getting them to dream with you may be the best way for them to see how it could actually work for the company.

INNOVATIVE MARKETING: CREATIVITY ON DISPLAY

Whether or not you can initiate an innovative marketing effort will depend on the imagination of your client and your passion for the innovative idea you are selling. **Whenever you are proposing a new idea that nobody in their market position has done before, you will understandably have to overcome objections.** How can you best do this?

- **Let your passion shine through.** Do not propose an innovative idea unless you are squarely behind it and believe it is absolutely right for the client. If you are insincere, and you are selling the idea for a reason that is suspect (say, for profit or further connections) the client will figure it out right away. You should believe in the idea so much that if you were in your client's shoes, you couldn't resist the idea and would gladly back it, despite the investment.

- **Have supporting information.** If you have examples of other companies that have successfully done similar initiatives, present those to the client. Include any evidence of success or metrics that you can find to prove the success of the initiative. The more facts you have, the less anxiety they will feel about taking the risk, and the more likely they will move forward with the idea.

- **Bring a plan.** Pie-in-the-sky ideas will not fly unless you have a vision and plan in place as to how the idea can be accomplished. The client will definitely ask you the question, "How?" Be prepared to answer it for all phases of implementing the innovative idea, including what labor you could provide to make it happen.

I find that innovative marketing ideas are the most fun to create and have unlimited potential for clients. It can even elevate them to a singular spot in the marketplace or even disrupt the industry. The sky's the limit with the right idea, the right passion, and the right organization!

CAUSE MARKETING: REACHING OUT TO MAKE A DIFFERENCE

Although almost all clients agree that doing a cause marketing initiative is a great thing for a company to do, not everyone gets on board. Why not? Sure, sometimes budget is an issue, or they can't agree on a certain charity or nonprofit partner to support. Typically, though, it's because the company is modest. They are hesitant to make their charitable contributions known in a promotional way.

I have found that most clients are already doing some form of cause marketing already. What they are typically missing is the communication piece to their clients, prospects, and public that tells others about their efforts. When we were hired as the public relations agency for an $80 million transportation company, we discovered that during every holiday season, the company leadership gave their employees time off to volunteer at a local food bank. Although some customers knew of this initiative, they had

shared this holiday tradition with very few other audiences. We were able to get them media coverage of their generosity on local television and radio stations. It increased their community good will and even contributed to their employee recruitment efforts by publicly positioning them as a caring and principled organization.

CONCLUSION

The important thing for any agency to understand is that there are multiple ways to integrate the Golden Five Framework into a client's marketing strategy. As long as all five are considered, you are on the right track. I believe that for optimal results, in the majority of cases, all of the Golden Five should be included in your client's marketing efforts, but as always, you must be led by the agency-client dance. Understanding what is important to your client is just as important as doing your research to learn which type of marketing will have the most impact.

I also must add that although we consider all five types of marketing for our clients, we never claim to be the only one to implement all aspects of the plan. I always say I come from a place of abundance when it comes to business. I believe there are enough businesses in need of marketing help in the world to support anyone who can bring ideas, resources, and expertise to their door. To that end, although my agency is full service, we do work with many strategic partners who perform specialized services for our clients on our behalf. Where our client needs help in an area that is not of our expertise, we partner with other firms who offer those services as their bread and butter. I recommend the same to you.

And there you have it. I hope the advice in this book has inspired you to achieve more as you serve nonprofit and for-profit organizations, think more creatively, and enjoy your work more in the process. Helping others with their marketing strategies since 2006 has been a tremendous honor for us and I wish you the best in your endeavors as well. From one marketing agency owner to another, may your success be (Golden) five-fold!

The Golden Five Framework will produce a fruitful, integrated marketing strategy for your clients.

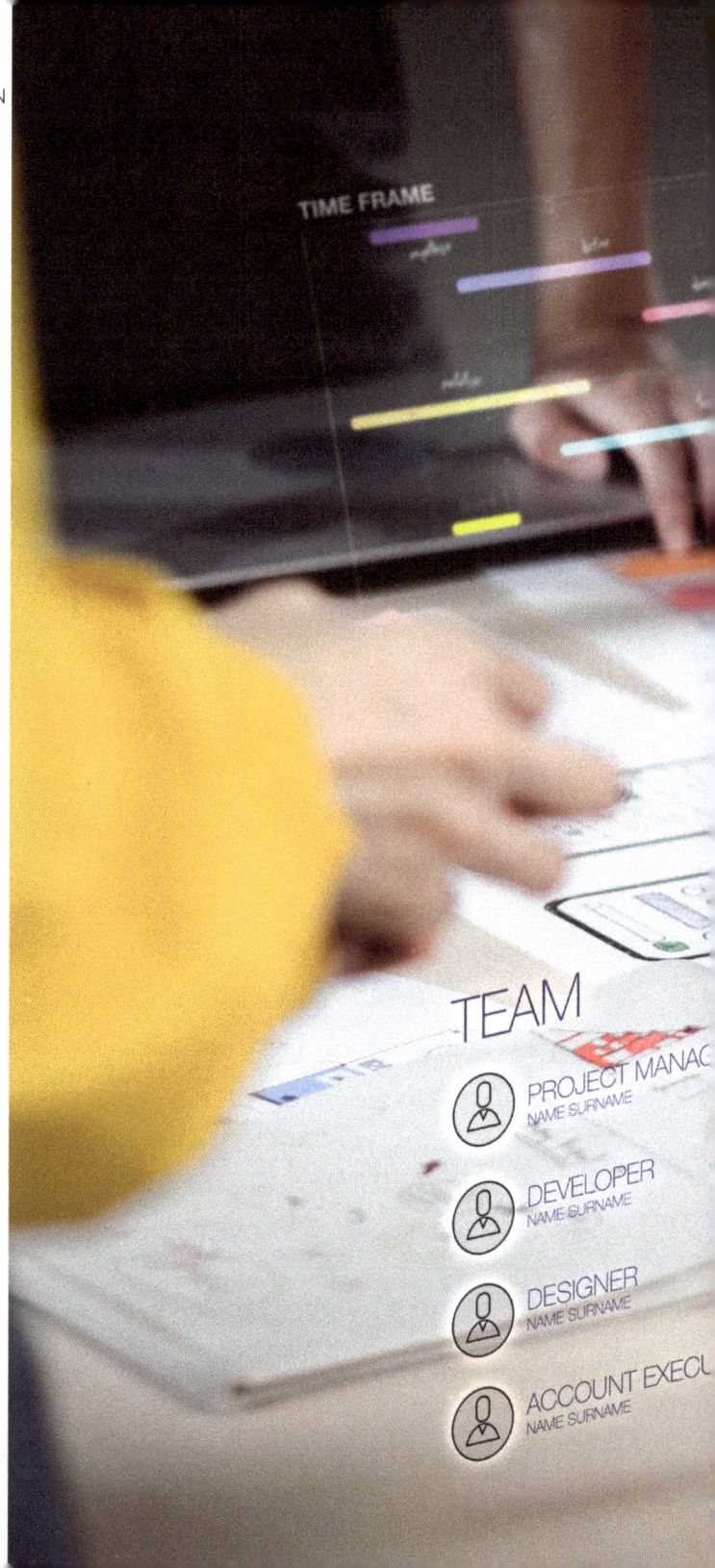

PART THREE

APPENDICES

DESIGN THINKING PROCESS

1 EMPATHIZE
2 DEFINE
3 IDEATION
4 PROTOTYPE
5 TEST
6 IMPLEMENT

ONLINE ASSESSMENT

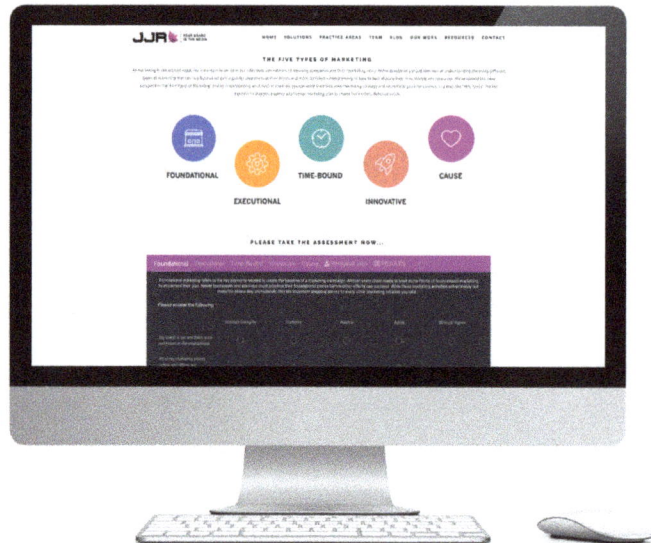

jjrmarketing.com/assessment

Here is a link to an online assessment that we provide to prospective clients at JJR Marketing to determine if and how they are currently using the Golden Five Framework in their business. Take it and use it to help businesses determine what area(s) of marketing they should focus on most.

QUICK GUIDE TO 5 TYPES OF MARKETING

Scan Code to Download

This guide encapsulates the 5 Types of Marketing in the Golden Five Framework and how to use them with your clients.

MARKETING CALENDAR TEMPLATE

Scan Code to Download

Get organized with your marketing efforts (or those of your client) with this marketing calendar template. It's guaranteed to get everyone on the same page.

JJR MARKETING ONLINE RESOURCES

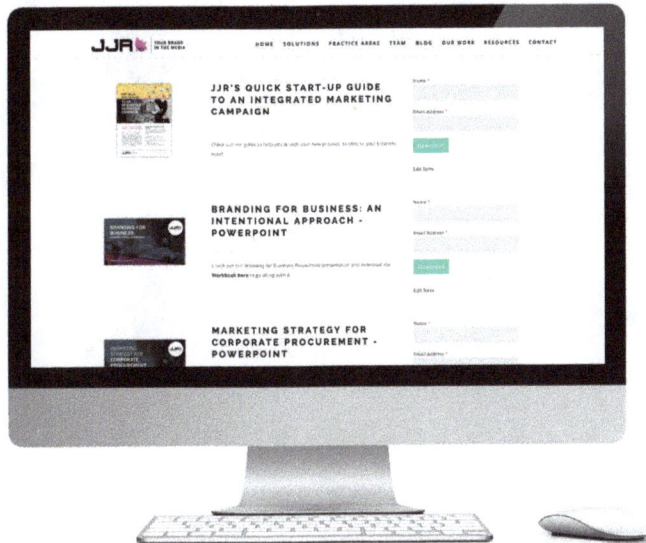

jjrmarketing.com/resources

Our resources page on the JJR Marketing website provides a valuable selection of tools to help you with the strategic function of creating a marketing plan and/or branding process for an organization, individual, or entrepreneur. Follow the link to access this amazing cache for your use.

ENDNOTES

A., Julija. 2022. smallbizgenius.net. April 22. Accessed April 27, 2022. https://www.smallbizgenius.net/by-the-numbers/small-business-statistics/#gref.

Amazon. 2021. Amazon VP of Worldwide Sustainability Kara Hurst Discusses Amazon's Latest Gender Equity Commitments . December 14.

Beasley, Charlette. 2021. Diversity in the Workplace Statistics: Why DEI Matters in 2022. December 22. Accessed June 18, 2022. https://fitsmallbusiness.com/dei-in-the-workplace/.

Brandwatch. n.d. "The Marketer of 2022." brandwatch.com. Accessed June 3, 2022. https://www.brandwatch.com/reports/marketer/view/.

Brown, Dave. 2021. Are Brochures Effective for Marketing in 2021? January 31. Accessed June 18, 2021. https://www.techsling.com/are-brochures-effective-for-marketing-in-2021/.

Business Insider. 2018. youtube.com. July 21. Accessed June 7, 2022. https://www.youtube.com/watch?v=iySnD19cN1s.

Chen, T., K. Fenyo, S. Yang, and J. Zhang. 2018. Thinking Inside the Subscription Box: New Research on E-commerce Consumers. February 9. Accessed June 17, 2022. https://www.mckinsey.com/industries/technology-media-and-telecommunications/our-insights/thinking-inside-the-subscription-box-new-research-on-ecommerce-consumers.

Comparably. 2021. comparably.com. November 17. Accessed June 6, 2022. https://www.comparably.com/news/best-brands-of-2021-according-to-gen-z-millennials/.

Comperatore, Elena, and Frederick Nerone. 2008. Coping with Different Generations in the Workplace. Journal of Business & Economics Research, 15-29.

CSR Journal. 2021. csrjournal.in. May 11. Accessed June 6, 2022. https://thecsrjournal.in/global-sustainability-report-google-carbon-neutral/.

D'Allegro, Joe. 2022. investopedia.com. May 2. Accessed June 6, 2022. https://www.investopedia.com/articles/investing/052014/how-googles-selfdriving-car-will-change-everything.asp#:~:text=The%20idea%20behind%20self%2Ddriving,to%20navigate%20to%20their%20destination.

Damianos, Giana. 2022. Essential sof Millennial Consumers . May 26. Accessed June 6, 2022. https://www.collagegroup.com/2022/05/26/essentials-of-millennial-consumers-2022/.

Danziger, Pam. 2021. therobinreport.com . November 15. Accessed June 6, 2022. https://www.therobinreport.com/why-amazon-has-a-hold-on-millennials/.

Fertik, Michael. 2019. How to Get Millenials to Trust and Respond to Your Advertising. February 14. Accessed June 6, 2022. https://www.forbes.com/sites/michaelfertik/2019/02/14/how-to-get-millenials-to-trust-and-respond-to-your-advertising/?sh=1cc37e836c81.

Forbes Agency Council. 2020. How to Bring a Brand to Life: 14 Lessons in Effective Storytelling. October 22. Accessed September 9, 2021. https://www.forbes.com/sites/forbesagencycouncil/2020/10/22/how-to-bring-a-brand-to-life-14-lessons-in-effective-storytelling/?sh=37bd03cd43cc.

Fourneau, Brecht. 2022. aventri.com. March 15. Accessed June 16, 2022. https://www.aventri.com/blog/event-marketing-trends-and-predictions.

Fry, Richard. 2020. Millenials Overtake Baby Boomers as America's Largest Generation. Retrieved from https://www.pewresearch.org/fact-tank/2020/04/28/millenials-overtake-baby-boomers-as-americas-largest-generation/

gettingattention.org. 2021. gettingattention.org. August 23. Accessed February 9, 2022. https://gettingattention.org/nonprofit-brand-mistake-komen-kfc/.

Gottlieb, Martin. 1986. Cashing in on a Higher Cause. July 6. Accessed February 9, 2022. https://www.nytimes.com/1986/07/06/business/cashing-in-on-higher-cause.html.

Haanaes, Knut. 2022. Why All Businesses Should Embrace Sustainability. May 9. Accessed June 18, 2022 from imd.org: https://www.imd.org/research-knowledge/articles/why-all-businesses-should-embrace-sustainability/

Hall, Tanya. 2018. The New 80/20 Rule of Social Media Marketing. Accessed September 21, 2021. https://www.inc.com/tanya-hall/the-new-80/20-rule-of-social-media.html.

He, Hongwei, Melody M. Chao, and Weichun Zhu. 2019. Cause-related Marketing and Employee Engagement: The Roles of Admiration, Implicit Morality Beliefs, and Moral Identity. February. Accessed February 10, 2022. https://www.sciencedirect.com/science/article/abs/pii/S0148296318304867.

Horne, Katie. 2021. digital.com. August 6. Accessed September 9, 2021. https://digital.com/small-business-statistics/.

hubspot.com. 2022. The Ultimate List of Marketing Statistics for 2022. Accessed June 16, 2022. https://www.hubspot.com/marketing-statistics.

Insider Intelligence. 2021. Podcast Industry Report: Market Growth and Advertising Statistics in 2022. July 29. Accessed September 23, 2021. https://www.insiderintelligence.com/insights/the-podcast-industry-report-statistics/.

Jacobson, Ben. 2019. martech.org. January 9. Accessed April 28, 2022. https://martech.org/hubspot-ceo-brian-halligan-reflects-on-the-evolution-of-inbound-marketing/.

Kaemingk, Diana. 2020. qualtrics.com. October 30. Accessed July 22, 2022. https://www.qualtrics.com/blog/online-review-stats/#:~:text=91%25%20of%2018%2D34%20year,reviews%20influenced%20their%20purchase%20decisions.

Karst, Tom. 2020. Cause Marketing is Win-Win for Companies and Charities, Speaker Says. March 2. Accessed February 9, 2022. https://www.producemarketguide.com/news/cause-marketing-win-win-companies-and-charities-speaker-says.

Korkki, Phylis. 2013. Need Motivation? Declare a Deadline. April 20. Accessed October 25, 2021. https://www.nytimes.com/2013/04/21/jobs/deadline-pressure-the-great-motivator.html.

Larson, Chris. 2016. Disruptive Innovation Theory: What it is and 4 Key Concepts. November 15. Accessed January 19, 2022. https://online.hbs.edu/blog/post/4-keys-to-understanding-clayton-christensens-theory-of-disruptive-innovation#:~:text=Disruptive%20innovation%20has%20been%20a,market%20can%20disrupt%20established%20businesses.

Lesonsky, Rieve. 2019. sba.gov. July 9. Accessed April 27, 2022. https://www.sba.gov/blog/how-get-most-your-marketing-budget.

Leswing, Kif. 2017. insider.com. September 15. Accessed April 27, 2022. https://www.insider.com/heres-what-google-looked-like-the-first-day-it-launched-in-1998-2017-9.

Lin, Ying. 2021. oberlo.com. July 4. Accessed April 27, 2022. https://www.oberlo.com/blog/online-review-statistics.

McKinsey & Company. 2021. Sign Up Now: Creating Consumer-and Business-Value with Subscriptions. May 26. Accessed June 17, 2022. https://www.mckinsey.com/business-functions/growth-marketing-and-sales/our-insights/sign-up-now-creating-consumer-and-business-value-with-subscriptions.

Meisenzahl, Mary. 2021. Businessinsider.com . August 15. Accessed September 9, 2021. https://www.businessinsider.com/dunkin-dropped-donuts-added-non-coffee-drinks-and-celebrity-partnerships-2021-8#dunkin-started-selling-the-charli-a-cold-brew-with-whole-milk-which-damelio-promoted-on-tiktok-dunkin-also-launched-a-merch-line-with-the-socia.

Melvin, Jemma. 2022. wyzowl.com. May 17. Accessed June 16, 2022. https://www.wyzowl.com/amazing-video-marketing-statistics/#:~:text=86%25%20of%20businesses%20use%20video%20as%20a%20marketing%20tool.,-It's%20clear%20that&text=It%20rose%20to%2063%25%20in,in%20our%20most%20recent%20survey.

Meng Zhu, Yang Yang, Christopher K Hsee. 2018. Journal of Consumer Research . February. Accessed October 22, 2021. https://academic.oup.com/jcr/advance-article-abstract/doi/10.1093/jcr/ucy008/4847790?redirectedFrom=fulltext.

Mental Health America. 2022. The State of Mental Health in America-2022 Key Findings. Report, Alexandria, VA: Mental Health America. p. 8. https://mhanational.org/sites/default/files/2022%20State%20of%20Mental%20Health%20in%20America.pdf

Mohsin, Maryam. 2020. 10 Branding Statistics You Need to Know in 2022. December 31. Accessed September 23, 2021. https://www.oberlo.com/blog/branding-statistics.

Molenaar, Koba. 2022. 20 Podcast Statistics You Should Know in 2022. May 3. Accessed June 17, 2022. https://influencermarketinghub.com/podcast-statistics/#:~:text=According%20to%20data%20shared%20by,over%20the%20last%2010%20years.

Motivate Design. 2017. How (RED) Made Their Mark and Stood the Test of Time. June 7. Accessed February 9, 2022. https://medium.com/@MotivateDesign/how-red-made-their-mark-and-stood-the-test-of-time-11d86d0136c8#:~:text=Since%20founded%2C%20(RED)%20has,marketing%20campaign%20%E2%80%94%20the%20color%20red.

Pew Research. 2014. pewresearch.org. March 11. Accessed April 27, 2022. https://www.pewresearch.org/internet/2014/03/11/world-wide-web-timeline/.

Pofeldt, Elaine. 2022. An Evolving Meetings Landscape. Meetings Outlook 2022 Spring Edition, Meeting Professionals International. https://www.mpi.org/docs/default-source/meetings-outlook/meetings-outlook-spring-2022.pdf

Porteous, Chris. 2021. 97% of Fortune 500 Companies Rely on Social Media. Here's How You Should Use it for Maximum Impact. March 18. Accessed September 22, 2022. https://www.entrepreneur.com/article/366240.

Porter Novelli/Cone. 2019. 2019 Porter Novelli/Cone Purpose Biometrics Study. Accessed February 10, 2022. https://www.conecomm.com/research-blog/purpose-biometrics.

Quah, Nick. 2021. 'Renegades' Podcast with Obama and Springsteen is Interesting . . . Enough. April 20. Accessed January 19, 2022. https://www.npr.org/2021/04/20/989084879/renegades-podcast-with-obama-and-springsteen-is-interesting-enoughhttps://www.npr.org/2021/04/20/989084879/renegades-podcast-with-obama-and-springsteen-is-interesting-enough.

Rathore, Sandeep. 2021. Content Marketing Statistics You Should Know. May 17. Accessed September 23, 2021. https://smallbiztrends.com/2020/11/content-marketing-statistics.html.

2020. reference.com. April 16. Accessed October 25, 2021. https://www.reference.com/history/invented-smart-goals-91a96ac7407ac68a.

Rist, Oliver. 2021. pcmag.com. September 7. Accessed April 24, 2022. https://www.pcmag.com/news/why-so-many-smbs-still-dont-have-websites.

Santora, Jacinda. 2022. Key Influencer Marketing Statistics You Need to Know for 2022. March 29. Accessed June 17, 2022. https://influencermarketinghub.com/influencer-marketing-statistics/.

Shepherd, Maddie. 2020. Crowdfunding Statistics (2021): Market Size and Growth. December 16. Accessed June 17, 2022. https://www.fundera.com/resources/crowdfunding-statistics.

2019. Sourcing Journal . September 3. Accessed September 9, 2021. https://sourcingjournal.com/topics/sustainability/qima-social-environmental-issues-165663/.

Stanton, Travis. 2019. The Statistics of Sponsorships. Research, Rochester, MN: Exhibitor Magazine. https://www.exhibitoronline.com/topics/article.asp?ID=2815

Sterling, Greg. 2018. martech.org. June 15. Accessed June 6, 2022. https://martech.org/report-52-of-millennials-want-retailers-to-mirror-their-values/.

2022. The Deloitte Global 2022 GenZ & Millennial Survey. Survey, deloitte.com. https://www2.deloitte.com/content/dam/Deloitte/at/Documents/human-capital/at-gen-z-millennial-survey-2022.pdf

Tulis, David. 2021. Latinas in Aviation Festival Recognizes Pioneering Women. October 6. Accessed January 19, 2022. https://www.aopa.org/news-and-media/all-news/2021/october/06/latinas-in-aviation-festival-recognizes-pioneering-women#:~:text=Latina%20pilots%20comprise%20about%201,pilots%20in%20the%20United%20States.

V., Ivana. 2022. Direct Mail Statistics That Will Have You Running to the Post Office . March 9. Accessed June 18, 2022. https://www.smallbizgenius.net/by-the-numbers/direct-mail-statistics/#gref.
wbdynamics.com. n.d. wbdynamics.com. Accessed June 7, 2022. https://www.wbdynamics.com/the-rise-of-corporate-social-responsibility/.

n.d. whoofey.com. Accessed April 27, 2022. https://whoofey.com/blog/how-many-ads-do-we-see-a-day-2021-ad-exposure/.

Wylonis, Christian. 2021. benefitspro.com. May 26. Accessed June 6, 2022. https://www.benefitspro.com/2021/05/26/millenials-are-all-in-on-transparency-and-companies-need-to-follow-suit/?slreturn=20220506145612.

Yahoo Small Business. 2014. 95% of Small Businesses Failed on Social Media. Accessed September 23, 2021. https://smallbusiness.yahoo.com/advisor/resource-center/95-small-businesses-failed-social-media-174753375/.

Zuckerman, Arthur. 2020. 82 Essential SEM Statistics: 2020/2021 Data, Trends & Predictions. May 27. Accessed September 23, 2021. https://comparecamp.com/sem-statistics/.

MARKETING
PUBLIC RELATIONS
CONTENT & CREATIVE

TAKING YOUR BUSINESS TO "ASCENDING" MODE, ITS OUR MISSION

JJR.
YOUR BRAND
IN THE MEDIA

ABOUT JJR MARKETING

For thought leaders seeking break through brand awareness, JJR is one of the fastest growing marketing and public relations agencies in Chicago, Illinois, with an international presence. We practice accountability that leads to high-performance results, extra value that leads to an enjoyable relationship, and a passionate perspective that leads to explosive creative. Every engagement is a mission to place a client's brand in the center of their most influential media creating buzz, leads, referrals, sales, growth and, at the end of the day, loyal brand advocates.

To learn more check out:
www.jjrmarketing.com

ABOUT THE AUTHOR

Jacqueline S. Ruiz is a visionary social entrepreneur that has created an enterprise of inspiration. With more than twenty years of experience in the marketing and public relations industry, she has created two successful award-winning companies, established two nonprofit organizations, published over 30 books, including the largest collection of Latina stories in a book anthology series in the world, and held events on four continents. She has received over thirty awards for her contributions and business acumen.

Jacqueline is the CEO of award-winning *JJR Marketing*, one of the fastest-growing top marketing and public relations agencies in Chicago, and *Fig Factor Media*, an international publishing services company that helps individuals bring their books to life. Jacqueline is also the founder of *The Fig Factor Foundation*, a not-for-profit organization dedicated to giving vision, direction, and structure to young Latinas ages twelve to twenty-five as well as the president of *Instituto Desarrollo Amazing Aguascalientes*, the first youth center in Calvillo, Aguascalientes, Mexico, offering various hands-on experiences, courses, and global connections to support the local troubled youth in defining their dreams.

Jacqueline serves as a board member for T*he Fig Factor Foundation*, the *World Leaders Forum*, and on the Alumni Executive Board at the *College of DuPage*. She is a recent graduate of the *DePaul University Women Entrepreneurship Cohort 3* and the *Stanford University Graduate School of Business*, *Latino Business Action Network Cohort 11*. Jacqueline is also one of the very few Latina sports airplane pilots in the United States and the founder of *Latinas in Aviation* global brand that now includes a book, magazine, scholarship, and events. She believes that *"taking off is optional, landing on your dreams is mandatory."*

www.ingramcontent.com/pod-product-compliance
Lightning Source LLC
Chambersburg PA
CBHW050344230326
41458CB00102B/6352